AUDREY COHEN COLLEGE LIBRARY
75 Varick St. 12th Floor
New York, NY 10013

Sunset over the Islands

The Caribbean in an Age of Global and Regional Challenges

F
2183
S48
1998

Sunset over the Islands

The Caribbean in an Age of Global and Regional Challenges

Andrés Serbin

St. Martin's Press
New York

AUDREY COHEN COLLEGE LIBRARY
75 Varick St. 12th Floor
New York, NY 10013

SUNSET OVER THE ISLANDS
© Copyright text 1998 by Andrés Serbin
© Copyright illustrations Macmillan Education Ltd 1998

All rights reserved. No part of this book may be used or reproduced in any manner whatsoever without written permission except in the case of brief quotations embodied in critical articles or reviews. For information, address:

St. Martin's Press, Scholarly and Reference Division,
175 Fifth Avenue, New York, N.Y. 10010.

First published in the United States of America in 1998

Printed in Hong Kong

Spanish edition published by Nueva Sociedad and INVESP.

ISBN: 0–312–21080–9

Library of Congress Cataloging-in-Publication Data
Serbin, Andrés
  Sunset over the islands: the Caribbean in an age of global and regional challenges / by Andrés Serbin.
      p.   cm.
  Includes bibliographical references and index.
  ISBN 0–312–21080–9 (cloth)
    1. Caribbean Area — Foreign relations — 1945–   2. Regionalism — Caribbean Area.   3. Association of Caribbean States.
  4. Competition, International.   5. Geopolitics — Caribbean Area.
  I. Titles.
F2183.S48   1997   97–38275
327.729—dc21   CIP

Cover illustration by Michael Bourne

Contents

Abbreviations	vii
Preface and acknowledgements	ix
Introduction	xv
Map – Caribbean Basin	xx

1 Perplexities and uncertainties – paradigms, ideas and maps in the global world — 1

- Globalisation, regionalisation, integration — 3
- The theoretical debate – between the *crisis of paradigms* and theoretical pluralism — 12
- Ideas, epistemic communities, traditions and state policies — 21
- Maps for navigation — 28

2 Crisis of identity and reconfiguration of the Caribbean Basin — 33

- The building of regional identities — 33
- Contemporary genealogy of the Caribbean Basin — 36
- Narratives, readings and reinterpretations — 40
- Toward the Greater Caribbean as a new founding myth? — 42

3 The globalising impact and regional reconfiguration — 47

- Economic globalisation — 47
- The socialisation of globalisation – state and civil society — 49
- Globalisation and regionalisation – the hemispheric effects — 52
- Regional security – the end of the geopolitical discourse as a regional catalyst — 56
- From geopolitical discourse to economic unease — 59
- The socio-political impact of globalisation and regionalisation — 65

4 The process of regionalisation in the Greater Caribbean — 71

- Intergovernmental regionalism – the Association of Caribbean States — 71
- Background to the creation of the ACS — 74
- Obstacles and difficulties in the configuration of the ACS — 79
- The social network of the regionalisation process in the Greater Caribbean — 82
- Transnational relations in the Greater Caribbean – the background — 86
- Transnational relations in the Greater Caribbean and the business sector — 88

Non-governmental organisations and alternative projects	89
The academic network and the emerging epistemic community	93
By way of preliminary conclusion	95

5 Towards an agenda for the Greater Caribbean – the exogenous and endogenous challenges   103

The challenge of globalisation – reconfiguration, competitive integration and security	105
The challenge of hemispheric polarisation	107
The challenge of heterogeneity and regional fragmentation	108
The political challenges of sovereignty, participation and representation	110
The social challenges – equity, employment, consumption and citizenship	113
The challenge of strengthening regional human resources – the creation of a regional epistemic community	114
By way of colophon	116

Bibliography   119

Index   133

Abbreviations

* Both abbreviations are used in the book and in the bibliography, depending on whether the items were published in Spanish or English.

ACE	Association of Caribbean Economists
ACS	Association of Caribbean States
ALADI	Asociación Latinoamericana de Integración (Latin American Association of Integration)
BLP	Barbados Labour Party
CAFRA	Caribbean Association for Feminist Research and Action
CAIC	Caribbean Association of Industry and Commerce
CARIBCAN	Canadian Cooperation Programme for the Caribbean
CARIBTAG	Caribbean Trade Advisory Group
CARICOM	Caribbean Community
CARIFORUM	Caribbean Forum with the participation of Haiti, Dominican Republic and CARICOM member states
CARIPEDA	Caribbean People's Development Agency
CCA	Caribbean Conservationist Association
CCAA	Caribbean/Central American Action Group
CCC	Caribbean Council of Churches
CEHI	Caribbean Environmental Health Institute
CEPAL*	Comisión Económica para América Latina y el Caribe (ECLAC in English)
C/LAA	Caribbean/Latin American Action Committee
CLACSO	Consejo Latinoamericano de Ciencias Sociales (Latin American Social Sciences Council)
CNHE	Consejo Nacional de Hombres de Empresa (National Council of Entrepreneurs)
CNIRD	Caribbean Network for Integrated Rural Development
COPPPAL	Comisión Permanente de Partidos Politicos de América Latina (Latin American Permanent Commission of Political Parties)
CPDC	Caribbean Policy Development Center
CRIES	Coordinadora Regional de Institutos de Investigaciónes Económicas y Sociales (Regional Coordination of Economic and Social Research Institutes)
CSA	Caribbean Studies Association

DAWN	Development Alternatives for Women Networks
ECLAC*	Economic Commission for Latin America and the Caribbean (CEPAL in Spanish)
FEDEPRICAP	Federación de Entidades Privadas de Centro América y Panamá (Federation of Private Entities of Central America and Panama)
FLACSO	Latin American Faculty of Social Sciences
FTAA	Free Trade Area of the Americas
GATT	General Agreement on Trade and Tariffs
ICIC	Iniciativa Civil para la Integración Centroamericana (Civil Initiative for Central American Integration)
INVESP	Instituto Venezolano de Estudios Sociales y Politicos (Venezuelan Institute of Social and Political Studies)
IS	Socialist International
MCCA	Mercado Común Centroamericano (Central American Common Market)
MERCOSUR	Mercado Común de América del Sur (South American Common Market)
NAFTA	North American Free Trade Agreement
NGO	Non-governmental organisation
ODCA	Organización Democráta – Cristiana de América Latina (Latin American Christian-Democrat Organization)
PNP	People's National Party
PNUMA	Programa de Naciones Unidas para el Medio Ambiente (UNEP in English)
PRI	Partido Revolucionario Institucional (Institutional Revolutionary Party)
PSOJ	Private Sector Organisation of Jamaica
SAFTA	South American Free Trade Area
SELA	Sistema Económico Latinoamericano (Latin American Economic System)
SIECA	Secretaría de la Integración Económica de Centroamérica (Central American Economic Integration Secretariat)
SICA	Sistema de Integración Centroamericana (Central American Integration System)
UNEP	United Nations Programme for the Environment (PNUMA in Spanish)
UNICA	Association of Caribbean Universities and Research Institutes
WAND	Women and Development
WTO	World Trade Organisation

Preface and acknowledgements

Confession is greater than any proof

Writing a book these days is a thankless task and perhaps has no more purpose than the mere exercise of writing it; the pure pleasure of doing it; for amusement; to put on paper the meditations of one's hours of work or leisure; or to group together some disordered ideas in a book with a cover. As everyone knows, for most people an image is worth a thousand words, especially in these days of television and the globalisation of information when few people appreciate reading – even the newspapers – and when books are being gradually displaced by computer screens and the Internet in a Gutenbergian shake-up of history.

Why then write a book – another book, so specific – on the Caribbean and globalisation, and perhaps too technical – to judge by much of the jargon used? Some say it is a need to be liked. Others assume that it is pure intellectual narcissism or even professional inertia. Others put it down to secret desires; to a yearning for transcendence; to a deliberate protest against the inexorable end that awaits us all – individually and collectively. Frankly, like this book, I offer no answers. On the contrary, questions abound. Having written and published, with moderate success, a number of books during my professional life, I believe there is no one single answer, but a combination of them. Some are explicit and fairly complicated – others are simpler and less obvious and others are unconfessable.

From a pragmatic point of view it is easier to meet the requirements of an academic career by publishing with some regularity, articles, chapters or papers in specialised journals and collective works in the conviction that, aside from professional advancement, in some unknown and devious manner, one is making a contribution to expanding knowledge of the human species. Not all of us can develop a theory of relativity, or contribute to a new quantum theory or to a theory of chaos or of the origin of the universe but we can console ourselves by thinking we leave behind some minimal contribution to the knowledge of the no less complex human nature and its workings in society.

More often than not in these partial attempts, probably insignificant and futile, we repeatedly fall back on collective responsibility, and alibis, when publishing. Nowadays collective works proliferate in the areas of what is called scientific knowledge – despite the postmoderns – to the detriment of individual works of longer gestation and even heavier weight which are difficult to tackle and digest in these days of instant trivia and fast food. Most collective volumes – and I have had the dubious honour of editing several of them – combine the efforts of a group of friends or colleagues with similar intellectual inclinations. They tend to be characterised by a tacit consensus, if not complicity, which makes them highly predictable and coherent. Exceptionally some collective works are noted for their incoherence, ambiguity and pluralist richness with a patchwork of contradictory, polemical and mutually critical not to say devastating points of view.

This book, despite being written by one person, belongs to the second category, without considering itself to be a small-scale sample of the chaos that supposedly surrounds us. It is certainly contradictory, plagued with omissions and personal inconsistencies and permeated more by questions and uncertainties than by clear answers. It reveals what, influenced by a wide range of experiences and reading, has stirred me to reflect on a subject of such special passion in my personal history – the Caribbean – a region which in its complexity has no shortage of doubts and uncertainties. Clearly this argument could be the perfect excuse for an incoherent book that affects to be multi-faceted and filled with apparently secret keys; a book that attributes the deficiencies of its structure and content to the nature of its subject of thought and study. I do not believe this is the case although it could be a partial justification for any defects. I do believe the book reflects the contradictions, ambiguities and multidimensional comings and goings of my own personality and experience – perhaps in empathy with the dynamic of the region itself; perpetually on parade and in movement; nomad from itself; shifting in its own identities.

I was born in Buenos Aires, a faraway city immersed in its own contradictions. My parents, expelled from Europe by the October Revolution and the Second World War, taught me to speak, feel, read and think in Russian and to celebrate baroque Orthodox rites in the gentle summers of the city on the river Plate. Thus during a great part of my adolescence I lived the ambiguity of belonging to two worlds, different and separate in distance and time, feeling comfortable in both. Perhaps this is what made me embark, with a degree of youthful folly, on the risky adventure of trying to change Argentina and if possible the world, swayed by the euphoria of May 1968 and the romanticism of Ché Guevara. I had the luck to get out unscathed, at least physically, and I reached Venezuela – a country of light and a different way of life where I learnt to see the world in other ways. In Venezuela I discovered, by physical absorption as much as by thought or discussion, the richness of the Caribbean and its people; a richness that extends beyond their languages, gods and customs. Early on I succumbed to the temptation to live it, think it and sometimes write about it.

Since that time, then, my world has been wider than a village or an island, but for that very reason many sided and changing, contradictory and far flung, difficult to pin down in a single phrase, paragraph, chapter or book. I have no regrets or complaints. It has been a life without too many certainties and with a heavy baggage of contradictions – an appropriate fate for any academic or intellectual worthy of the name. I do not consider for one moment, that my experiences are unique. I firmly believe they are typical of the world of modernity in which we have to live – in this I agree with Giddens (1993). It is a world where closed communities or villages or islands tend to disappear, dislocated by the spatial and temporal changes, the shifts and uprooting of an age of globalisation and rapid transformation where there is little room for the predominantly lineal and unidimensional certainties of other times.

This book is a reflection of these ambiguities and contradictions and is based on selected writings of recent years on the Caribbean – the object of a not totally consummated but enduring passion. I have tried to organise the chapters – updating and deepening some topics, deriving others, touching on yet others – in an effort to explain how change is affecting an archipelago of islands, isthmuses and divided territories confronted by the need to learn new rules in the face of the avalanche of global homogenisation. I will be satisfied if someone, with a reasonable dose of patience, reads a few fragments and reflects on the future of the Caribbean. Perhaps the only justification for this book is to give continuity to an interest and a preoccupation – not to say love affair – for the region which goes back over two decades, the key achievements of which have been recorded at various times in many different publications. It was also written as a response to the many stimuli that have nourished this interest during my academic life. For this reason the book responds not only to multiple intertextualities – as the postmodernists like to say – but also to influences, interconnections and emotions experienced during the journey that I began as an anthropologist, which later developed an interdisciplinary perspective and now embraces international relations and political science in general, with traces of sociology, history and even social psychology. It encompasses the diverse rites of passage and initiation I have survived at different stages and in different cultural and disciplinary contexts both within the region and outside it. With all its unevenness, the book is an attempt to answer some of the questions, critical commentaries and debates to which I have been subjected by academics and students, not to mention political decision makers, government officials and businessmen at national and regional level. Its aim is not only to be widely read but to bring together, in the simplest and most accesible manner within the author's limitations, some of the theoretical debates currently in progress and the questions and uncertainties imposed on the region by global changes.

Some of the ideas in this book originated directly or indirectly in discussions with friends – equally or even more fascinated by the region – who, over the years, have stimulated, questioned and debated some of the arguments developed here but whom I will save from the embarrassment of being named. They know who they are and know that they can begin 'sharpening their critical knives' for the debate on the ideas put forward here, as they usually do. Many of the works that have inspired parts of this book were originally published as chapters of collective volumes or as articles in specialised journals, or presented as papers in conferences and symposia. In these cases I have identified the sources although the original ideas have suffered later mutations and alterations. Some of the ideas and their permutations and derivations, have sprung from courses and seminars I have given in the Central University of Venezuela, mainly in the Postgraduate School in Social Sciences, as well as in universities, research centres and think-tanks in the Caribbean, Latin America, the United States of America (US), Canada and Europe.

Contrasting intellectual environments have also made a variegated and superimposed contribution to stimulating different interpretations of regional developments in both theory and practice. In this, as usual, having time available to read, think and talk with people related to the field has been fundamental. In this respect I am especially grateful for the fortunate coincidence of a sabbatical leave from my teaching activities at the Central University of Venezuela, the award of a Fulbright research scholarship and an invitation from the Center for International Affairs of the University of Harvard (CFIA), which allowed me to spend ten months in the stimulating environment of Cambridge, Massachusetts delving into libraries, taking part in seminars and workshops and, above all, reading voraciously. Here, I owe special thanks to Jorge Dominguez, the director of the CFIA, for his support.

I have a very special debt to Yolanda and Daniel van Eeuwen at the University of Aix-en-Provence, for their invitation to round off those ten months with a month in France, where I gave an intensive course on the theory of international relations in the Doctorate of

Political Sciences and for their warm hospitality and stimulating conversation during my stay. After ten months of austere, frugal and productive academic life supporting the impositions of neopuritan *political correctness* in New England, one month of spring in the south of France, shared between teaching, writing, debating and gastronomic explorations, provided the necessary balance which restored a degree of good sense to this project.

I must make a special mention of the help and tolerance of my colleague and friend Francine Jacóme, who took over the directorship of INVESP during my leave of absence, and of the patience with which the researchers and the staff of that institution provided me with information, bibliography and backing from Venezuela and during my frequent visits to Caracas.

Undoubtedly this whole process imposed a heavy burden on my family who accompanied me and helped me during the period away from Venezuela. Without them and their unwavering support, the separation, however productive, would have been difficult to bear.

Thanks to this period of intellectual enrichment and stimulation in such contrasting surroundings and to this combination of support and stimuli, I was able to organise the articles, papers and essays on the region which I had published in specialised journals and collective works over the last five years – a period rich in changes and drastic transmutations in the international system. I also took on the task of adding new ideas and approaches and, essentially, trying to give an appearance of coherence to my research in the context of the programmes of INVESP in the hope that this book may serve as both a draft and a prologue for the project on regionalism and civil society in Latin America and the Caribbean, in which I am currently involved. All this was made possible by a generous contribution from the Ford Foundation and the support of the Latin American Economic System.

Last but not least, I owe a special thanks to Gabriel Dobson, for his skilful assistance in preparing an English version of this book.

Cambridge, Massachusetts, 1994–1995/Caracas, 1995–1996

Introduction

'I have nothing to offer except a way of looking at things'
Erik H. Erikson, 1986

Recent trends and changes in the international system have not only marked the dynamic of international relations at the global, hemispheric and regional levels, but have also created a crisis in the traditional paradigms of interpretation and theoretical analysis of international relations; in particular, from a global standpoint, the validity of regional or area studies is being questioned and interest in them has declined.

The end of the Cold War and the bipolar world, combined with the transformation and fragmentation of the USSR and Eastern Europe, put an end to the area studies that were favored by the US academic establishment. Sovietology (cf. King, 1994) and Sovietologists have had to disperse in search of new academic niches in order to survive. With all the differences of scale and strategic priorities, a similar situation is affecting *Caribbeanists* who specialise in that subregion of the Western Hemisphere. The eclipse of the geostrategic importance of the Caribbean Basin, particularly for the traditional extra-regional actors such as the former European metropolises and the US in the aftermath of the end of the Cold War, has caused a similar exodus of analysts and academics from Caribbean studies, especially in universities and research centres in the industrialised countries. Yet global interdependence and systemic generalisations cannot conceal the need for area studies based on a deep knowledge of the languages, cultures and politics of a specific region, particularly in the case of such a complex and heterogeneous region as the Caribbean.

After the Second World War the Caribbean witnessed the development of studies which became progressively disassociated from the ethnocentrism that characterised progress in the Western sense but which benefited from the advances in theory and methodology made by Western social sciences (Maingot, 1983a, 3). In turn the linguistic, cultural and political diversity of the Caribbean Basin required the development of interdisciplinary studies or at least the growing use of multidisciplinary paradigms (ibid.), which eventually even led to an extradisciplinary approach (Sankatsing, 1994) to deal with the region's heterogeneity.

Over the last fifty years, the Caribbean Basin (including Central America and the South American Caribbean countries) has stimulated an accumulation of specific research (Serbin, 1987, 27–30) and a proliferation of research centres involved in studies of different aspects of the region (located both inside and outside the region and focusing on the Caribbean islands and Cuba as well as on Central America). This process has been accompanied by the emergence and growth of networks of researchers and professional associations involved in the study of the Caribbean. As a result despite the recent loss of prestige of area studies, there persists a conceptual, theoretical, institutional and disciplinary interest in the region which responds to the dictum that 'research, unlike speculation, requires an objective place' (Wood, 1974, 524). The conceptual, theoretical, institutional and disciplinary differences created by this activity reflect the complexity of the region and the need for an anchor in this age of spatial and temporal dislocation.

Despite the globalising winds that are homogenising the world and the proliferation of comparative studies, especially in sociology and political science, there persists an accumulated body of research and studies and an interest in regional situations which is out of step with the present apparent lack of academic interest in area studies. A glance at the bibliography at the end of this book is enough to illustrate the abundance of material on the region published in recent years. It is becoming evident that, beyond domestic political, economic and cultural factors, globalisation is very much conditioned by geographical conditions and regional differences. Aside from its clear identification with the expansion and transformation of contemporary capitalism, globalisation finds different expressions in Europe, Japan and North America and more recently in the periphery (Albert, 1993). Hence two sets of variables need to be emphasised; the regional with its particularities and the international. These variables create a specific intersecting space in the dynamic of certain distinctive geographical areas (Stallings, 1995, 1–2), such as the Caribbean.

The *crisis of paradigms* which has recently marked the discussion on approaches and theoretical perspectives in international relations, has exposed the need to redirect area studies and include novel interpretative schemes to account for the growing complexity, rapid change and diversity of the international system. The *third wave* of the debate on international relations has questioned the realist and neorealist assumptions, particularly present in the geostrategic interpretation of the regional dynamic and has led to the growing importance of pluralist neoliberal, globalist and reflectivist approaches in the interpretation of the processes of subregional integration, of linkage between external pressures and the domestic demands of Caribbean societies and in the emergence of new actors and new issues on the regional agenda. The consequent changes of approach and perspective in the analysis of the region, with growing emphasis on its international components, are related to significant changes in the perceptions of the regional actors in government, business, intergovernmental and non-governmental organisations and in the social and political sectors of each society. The conceptualisations and definitions of the region are in the throes of transformation, as are the role and dynamic of the interactions of the protagonists in relation to the issues and priorities on the regional agenda. Regional projects and orientations are emerging and fostering a new kind of regionalism with distinctive features in a context of rapid change and an increasingly complex subregional dynamic.

Paradoxically, the *regional imaginary* created by this process and the economic, political, social and symbolic initiatives that nourish and sustain it, are at once differentiated, linked and eventually blended into the process of world globalisation. This occurs in the context of the contradictions imposed on the respective identities by the linkage between the processes of globalisation and regionalisation; the re-definition of the functions of the state, of the scope of the nation state and of the different kinds of nationalism – national, ethnic, religious, regional; and the particularities of the ongoing renewal of the role of civil society in the processes of democratic governance. As a result the Caribbean Basin has once more become a sounding board for the dynamics of the international system based, however, on its own particular historical evolution and cultural configuration. At the same time the region is articulating responses and strategies to deal with exogenous pressures and demands which are not always coherent or effective in meeting the challenge of global transformation.

From this perspective, apart from being an attempt to rekindle a debate on the importance of an approach based on the study of the Caribbean as an area, this book is an effort to analyse the new processes that are defining the identity and differentiability of the subregion in a world in transformation. It speculates about the outlook for the Caribbean Basin in the coming years; about the sense of insularity that geographically and culturally characterises a large part of it; and about the impact of globalisation not only on the productive, commercial and financial dimensions but also on the geopolitical, sociopolitical, cultural and ideological components. Hopefully, the result is a fresh look at the region based on a new dialogue between a changing reality and the ideas that are striving to comprehend it, especially from the standpoint of the discipline of international relations. It is also a response to the dynamic imposed by the region's own actors – unlike the definitions *from outside* which have characterised it in the past – from the perspective of an informed view of the world dynamic that is shaping the region and the ideas and conceptual maps that contribute to its interpretation.

The book is also an attempt to formulate questions about the region's future in the framework of global transformation and not necessarily to make predictions and prognostications. More than a discussion on all the possible scenarios, it is an effort to identify the challenges that the new global situation imposes by outlining an agenda that responds to change. In this sense it is not a definitive text but a compendium of the doubts and questions that have plagued the author's works on the region over the last five years and which he believes could be of some use as a blueprint and a menu of perplexities – rather than a manual of certainties – in the continuing debate on the future of the Caribbean Basin.

As Erik Erikson said, 'I have nothing to offer except a way of looking at things', however fragmentary and dispersed although not for that of less consequence.

xx *Map – Caribbean Basin*

1 | Perplexities and uncertainties – paradigms, ideas and maps in the global world[1]

'The map is not the territory'
        Alfred Korzbyski

The Caribbean Basin is gradually emerging from an historical genesis that was marked by colonialism; by a regional configuration forged by an exogenous economic and geopolitical dynamic; by the vicissitudes imposed by its ethnic, cultural, linguistic and religious fragmentation; and by the consequent proliferation of actors and identities. With the end of the Cold War and the bipolar world, and with increasing pressure to adapt to a global system characterised by competitive and efficient economic integration, a new chapter is beginning in the contemporary history of the region. Many questions are emerging on the possibilities of reshaping the region in terms of new regional and international parameters, on its future in a changing international system and on its real capacity for dealing with the new global challenges. The recent creation of the Association of Caribbean States (ACS) is a breakthrough to a new stage which is, however, marked by the perplexities and uncertainties of changing referential frameworks and by new demands and complex international processes in the throes of transformation. These perplexities and uncertainties themselves mark the development of interpretations of these transformations and their impact on the region as well as the formulation of responses aimed at ensuring the survival of the states and societies of the Caribbean Basin in an increasingly competitive and voracious international system.

    Written from the perspective of these perplexities and uncertainties, this book is an attempt to trace a referential base for understanding the transformation of the region and the alternatives for its future. We will describe and analyse the regional processes in progress in the context of the disjunctive created by global changes and open new areas of debate on scenarios for the Caribbean. To do this it is fundamental, from a holistic and integrated perspective, to begin by tracing some of the conceptual elements that may act as a guide for the description and analysis of the regional transformation and to establish some theoretical premises as the underlying thread of this book. We do not claim to have an answer to all the concerns expressed, particularly in the ongoing debate and in what is called the 'crisis of paradigms' in international relations. Such a purpose is quite beyond this brief and modest review of the processes under way in the Greater Caribbean and their relationship to global change. Yet, in spite of the inherent limitations of this kind of initiative – to which we will return shortly – we believe this work can be a starting point for an organised and systematic debate on the region's future and on the policies needed to prepare effective and operational responses to the transformations taking place in the international system, while never losing sight of a much broader and all inclusive dynamic.

From this perspective the recent transformations in the international system and their impact on the Caribbean Basin, open up three fundamental conceptual questions from the regional standpoint on the broader issues created by the dynamic of the system.

The first question is, 'What is the regional capacity for responding to these changes?' This can be examined in terms of four main areas of action. The first is the economic-productive area – commerce, finance and technology, efficiency and competitiveness in an international order characterised by asymmetric interdependence and inequality. The second area is geopolitical – capacity for collective regional political and diplomatic response; creation of appropriate institutions and systems; deepening of regional integration and the regionalisation process. The third area of action is socio-political – capacity to mobilise more than just the political and economic elite around a regional project; capacity to generate development strategies based on regional cooperation with the inclusion of broad sectors of the population; mechanisms for participation by the social actors involved; establishment of democratic mechanisms for decision making. The fourth area of action is the symbolic – generation of a regional project with its own ideology; promotion and development of a social imaginary based on communality rather than differences, overcoming the negative social and ethnic barriers and categorisations that have been inherited and recreated in the region; creation of an inclusive regional identity based on the process of regional integration and regionalisation.

The response to this first question has to be preceded by a discussion of the scope of the concepts of globalisation, integration and regionalisation in the context of contemporary changes.

The second question for the elite and for a varied group of emerging social actors is, 'What theoretical paradigms can the social sciences offer – especially involving international relations – as a satisfactory interpretation of global and regional transformation and for use as interpretative schemes and conceptual maps for debating and implementing regional initiatives?' To create an holistic and integrated perspective, input is required from the current debate on the limitations and scope of the theoretical paradigms, particularly from the field of international relations but also from other disciplines. But at the same time the economic, political and especially socio-historical particularities of regional societies have to be identified and taken into account. This is why a presentation is needed of the present scope of the theoretical debate in the field of international relations and the social sciences as the outline of a conceptual and theoretical guide for this book.

The third question relates to the capacity of the economic and political elite of Caribbean Basin societies, particularly the academic and intellectual elite, to link the ideas from the previous debate with the formulation and implementation of specific initiatives and policies, in an effort to build a regional consensus on the most urgent and basic needs and on the measures needed to deal with them. The question is, 'Is there a real possibility that the intellectual models and traditions that characterise the region's links between the production of ideas and the economic, political and social reality, are capable of generating the inputs needed to transform and adapt society to the new global conditions in the economic, political, social and cultural spheres?' The answer requires a discussion of how intellectuals and academics relate to the world of the political decision-makers and of the real influence of ideas and theoretical approaches on international processes without, however, neglecting to analyse the relationship of these academics and intellectuals with the rest of civil society and their interests and aspirations at regional level.

This set of three problematical, conceptual and theoretical questions serves as a guide for the construction of a conceptual framework for a 'theoretically-informed empirical analysis' (Stubbs and Underhill, 1994, 24) before the analysis of the processes that characterise regionalisation in the Caribbean Basin. This is the theme of this introductory chapter.

Globalisation, regionalisation, integration

In the wake of global changes and the *crisis of paradigms*, a wide ranging debate has developed on the concept of *globalisation* and its scope and limitations. Apart from it having become a buzz word used indiscriminately by the media, in the analyses of international experts and in the discourses of politicians, the globalisation debate reveals a preoccupation with the state of things, with a series of processes and a set of perceptions on the contemporary world and the transformations it is undergoing. In part the debate is about the validity of viewing the globalisation process as peculiar to our era or whether, on a different scale and in different historical conditions, there have always been forms of interconnection and interaction between the societies, peoples and states of the planet, through trade, political alliances or conflicts, or the spread of ideas and technological innovations (Buzan, 1991).

What is different is that the globalisation process that began with the expansion of Western capitalism and the growing interdependence of societies after the closing stages of the Second World War, involves ever more complex interconnections and interactions between states, societies and multidimensional groups. The emerging networks and connections are not restricted to a particular field – trade, communications or the spread of ideas and values – but embrace a complex web of transactional links and coordination. From this standpoint, contemporary globalisation embraces two distinct phenomena. Firstly, political, economic and social activity acquires a global character and reach. Secondly, there is 'an intensification of the levels of interaction and interconnection between states and societies which creates an international society' (Held, 1991, 206). In fact what is new in the modern global system is the 'chronic intensification of patterns of interconnection, dominated by phenomena such as the modern communications industry and information technology, and by the spread of globalisation through new dimensions of interconnection – technological, organisational, administrative and legal, among others – each of which has its own logic and its own dynamic of change' (ibid.). In short, globalisation has meant that practically all the societies and states on the planet have been rapidly affected by a series of economic, political and cultural developments from other parts of the world, which has become 'one single world' (Parry, 1994, 1).

Essentially this perspective highlights the role of globalisation in the economic, political and social interpenetration of the societies of the planet, with effects on the creation of a broader, less structured and more complex international agenda, incorporating a much more diffuse range of interests and a much more extensive team of actors than in the past, no longer reduced exclusively to nation states. This situation has lead to the flowering of 'numerous spheres, sets or circuits that operate around the agenda, the agents, the scenarios and the resources of power, and which link in a variety of ways the different sectors of national societies through their specific interests' (Tomassini, 1989, 25–6). Yet globalisation is frequently perceived in terms of its predominantly economic dimension, primarily as a description of how the large corporations have organised themselves into global networks of services and information and have set up a global system of cooperation and competition which they use to divide up sectors of trade and industry by means of direct foreign investment and information technology (Badie and Smouts, 1992, 202).

Critical voices have surfaced which say that this predominantly economic approach 'hinders and limits the apprehension of other facets (political, cultural, etc.)' and often 'distorts the role that economic globalisation can play in development processes by overvaluing the positive aspects and minimising or ignoring the negative aspects of its capacity to transform' (Moneta, 1994, 147). This view emphasises the role of certain actors, such as multinational enterprises and financial agents, as the principal agents of globalisation (ibid., 148)[2].

The more eminently political views of the globalisation process emphasise the impact of economic globalisation and the expansion of transnational forces and interactions. They stress the difficulties in establishing an international order between nations and the effect of globalisation on the traditional roles of states, the concept of the nation state and the limits of national sovereignty (Held, 1991; Parry, 1994). They point to the effect of globalisation on the configuration of *one-world politics* or *world politics* or *global politics* (McGrew and Lewis, 1992). To a greater or lesser extent these approaches use the theoretical arsenal of the disciplines of political economy and international relations. They assume a greater or lesser linkage in the processes of interdependence which globalisation generates between international economic agents and market forces on the one hand, and political actors, chiefly the state, on the other. The political considerations of the globalisation process encompass the spread of the Western version of democracy and its connection with development; the problem of governance, representativeness and world political legitimacy; and the emergence of global or regional systems and institutions which provide legitimate forums in the dynamic of international relations (Held, 1991; Diamond, 1994; The Commission of Global Governance, 1995).

The economic and political view of globalisation identifies five distinctive characteristics, following Frankel (1988). These are (1) the growing complexity and diversity of the world system; (2) intense patterns of interaction; (3) extreme permeability of the nation state; (4) rapid cascading change; and (5) the fragility of international order and governance in conditions of increasing economic interdependence (McGrew, 1992b, 313). Rosenau's analysis of global turbulence provides some additional characteristics namely the proliferation of actors; impact of dynamic technologies; globalisation of national economies; emergence of interdependent or transnational issues; weakening of states and restructuring of loyalties; subgroupism; and the expansion of hunger, poverty and the Third World (Rosenau, J., 1992c).

Other approaches to globalisation emphasise the cultural dimension imposed by the globalisation of communications as part of the information revolution – the standardisation of advertising messages and habits of consumption, and the promotion of Western values such as democracy and human rights – with their effects on the development of global homogenisation and which could eventually dilute local and national particularities and affect national, ethnic and religious identities. Versions with a more marked social bent, particularly following the Stockholm Social Development Summit, focus on the formation of a global or planetary society and the emergence of global issues including environmental problems; demographic expansion with its aftermath of migration, joblessness and poverty; the emergence of terrorism and drug trafficking; and the spread of epidemics across the world (Club of Rome, 1991).

Yet in general two elements tend to be emphasised in the analysis of the globalisation process, whether in terms of a specific dimension – economic, political, cultural, communicational or social – or of a multi-dimensional approach. The first element, either implicit or explicit, is *globalisation from above*, which is based on the role of multinational corporations, the more developed and powerful states and the world's political and economic elite in a context of asymmetries and inequalities of all kinds. The second is the essentially homogenising character of the process, to the point of creating visions of a world made uniform by the complex interweaving of all the multiple dimensions of globalisation. In this context, globalisation tends to generate opposition forces which can increase the fragmentation of the world system of states and societies, since growing interconnections and mutual awareness create the conditions for the emergence of conflicts and tensions based on opposing interests, values and perceptions. This leads us to McGrew's view that globalisation should be conceived of as a dialectic process or a set of interrelated processes, which have a highly unequal and differentiated impact on societies and political spheres (McGrew, 1992a, 23).

In an attempt to systematise the complexity and the dynamism of the changes brought about by these process, Rosenau refers to the macro-parameter formed by the distribution of power in world politics through which states, international organisations and other important actors interact. This marks a bifurcation of global structures between, on the one hand, the original state-centred world of sovereign nation states and the structures they impose in terms of hegemony, bipolarity or multipolarity; and, on the other, a complex multicentric world shaped by the interactions of relatively autonomous and heterogeneous actors comprising multinational corporations, ethnic minorities, subnational governments and bureaucracies, professional associations, political parties, transnational organisations and others. In this sense, the bifurcation, while not implying the disappearance of states as key actors on the international system, does lead to a global *turbulence* characterised by the complex and fast-moving dynamic of the globalisation process with the participation of new actors and spaces and circuits of interaction (Rosenau, 1990; 1992c).

Doubts have also been expressed about the *world order* imposed by the protagonists of globalisation – whether multinational corporations, industrialised states or the transnational economic and political elite. On the other hand a critical approach postulates *globalisation from below* promoted by a set of transnational forces animated by a concern for the environment, human rights, gender and the solidarity of different cultures merged in an effort to eliminate poverty, oppression, exclusion and collective violence, by creating a 'world community' based on a global civil society (Brecher et al., 1993, ix)[3]. From this point of view the promoters of *globalisation from below* through the development of a global citizenship, question the homogenising and consumerist trends of *globalisation from above* and its vision of the world as an 'homogenising supermarket for those with purchasing power, while those without financial resources are excluded and, possibly, suppressed by police, paramilitary or military means' (Falk, 1993, 50). While recognising the existence of conflicts and contradictions between the different versions of *globalisation from below*, the predominant trend is to conceive the formation of a unifying global civil society built on non-governmental organisations, social and gender movements, ethnic and religious minorities, and political, environmental and radical groups, which oppose the development of a globalisation process fundamentally driven by transnational corporations, international financial organisations and the governments of the most powerful states which receive most of the benefits of the process.

The emergence of social movements and non-governmental organisations since the 1970s, in both the industrialised and developing worlds, and their criticism of the traditional political parties and the role of elite in government, coupled with a reassessment of the role of civil society – and possibly of the business and political elite concerned by the reduction and redefinition of the role of the state especially in the development of social and redistribution policies – has led to the development of this view at international level and to the creation of supporting links and transnational networks. Frequently, however, the *globalisation from below* view loses sight of some of the negative aspects of the emerging transnational civil society, such as organised transnational crime, international terrorism and the emergence of particularistic fundamentalism. These dubious aspects of global civil society which are benefiting from financial globalisation and the information revolution in the framework of *globalisation from below*, also challenge the dynamic of the globalisation process (The Commission on Global Governance, 1995, 10). For all that it is possible to argue the need for a dialectic approach that unites both types of globalisation in a view that is interactive rather than dichotomous.

These critical views are accompanied by emerging *particularistic reactions* on the international scene which are asserting themselves on the cultural and religious level, in response to the homogenising mechanisms of globalisation. These reactions generate forms of cultural confrontation that could replace the ideological antagonism of the Cold War as the articulating mechanism of the international dynamic (Huntington, 1993; Badie and Smouts, 1992). On a more economic and political level, they could also bring about *regionalisation* processes in an bid to optimise the actions of societies in specific geographical areas in the presence of the challenge of globalisation. These particularistic reactions have ethnic, national or religious bases ranging from the rise of Islamic fundamentalism to the versions of ethnic and religious nationalism that sustain radical movements in the countries that emerged from the collapse of the socialist camp, especially in Eastern Europe. As these movements are more relevant to other regions than to Latin America and the Caribbean, let us leave, for the time being, their discussion to concentrate on the regionalisation process.

In the context of the dynamic of globalisation, an intensifying regionalisation process is identifiable which, in its more empirical forms, has created a triad of foci of economic dynamism in North America, the European Union and the Asia-Pacific rim with its hub in Japan[4]. The triad, which is interconnected by the convergence of global economic and political interests, is generating other regionalisation processes as a reaction to the internal and external challenges of global transformation and the possible emergence of a world fragmented by the protectionist and concentrationist practices of these economic-political blocs. A case in point is the regionalisation process in Latin America and the Caribbean to which we will return later with special emphasis on the Caribbean Basin.

Far from being contradictory and antagonistic to the ongoing globalisation process, some analysts are convinced that regionalisation is a logical reaction because it uses and organises globalisation as part of its own dynamic (Badie and Smouts, 1992, 203). Within this dialectic the regionalisation process is characterised by its own dynamism, created by geographical limits, trade and capital flows, differentiated values and identities marked by specific situations (Whiting, 1993, 19)[5]. It is taking place in a clear referential framework, frequently of a reactive-defensive nature, in the context of globalisation and the phenomenon of the formation of regional economic and political blocs. Yet, as Mols rightly points out, a distinction has to be made between regionalism and regional integration. Regionalism is based on identifiable geographical areas and common concerns – whether external, such as the potential threat of marginalisation from the international economic system, or internal, such as the identification of common domestic interests. It is a relatively vague conceptualisation particularly in relation to cultural and psychosocial identity. In contrast the idea of regional integration is a highly technical concept with an inherent ambiguity in the relationship between the process and the result (Mols, 1993, 54–5).

Regional integration, particularly on the economic level, responds to two concepts. The first, which is conceptually associated with the neofunctionalist approach and empirically with the European integration process, relates to the institutional merger of two or more political entities in a new, more extended entity. This concept emphasises the federal aspirations of the integration process; the hypothesis of supranationality based on the progressive transfer of national sovereignty and political integration – the spill-over of the economic into the political sphere. It accepts the fundamental role of the interpenetration of bureaucracies and the learning process of the elite as protagonists in the growth of cooperation that is likely to end in the transfer of national sovereignty for the sake of the federal ideal (Mitranyi, 1965, 123–4, and 1943; Haas, E., 1964). Although many of its assertions have been toned down and questioned by the empirical development of European integration, that approach is a fundamental conceptual reference in the analysis of regionalisation and integration processes (cf. Dougherty and Pfaltzgraff, 1990, 431–67; Allum, 1995).

The second concept, going beyond a predominantly institutional view, emphasises a deepening pragmatic integration through economic cooperation between countries in the context of world changes, particularly by the creation of forms of economic integration – free trade areas, customs unions, common markets, economic unions and total economic integration (Balassa, 1980, 2). Integration is not merely reduced to intergovernmental cooperation; it involves the creation of a new entity or regional economic unit as an organised framework for accommodation between member states on the exchange of goods, services, capital and people (Smith, 1993, 5)[6]. In Latin America the theoretical bases of this concept with their evolution into a more pragmatic view – which we will analyse later under open regionalism – are found in the works of ECLAC (CEPAL) beginning in the 1960s (Guerra-Borges, 1991, 136–51). The concept has taken on special importance with the reactivation and acceleration of subregional integration processes in Latin America and the Caribbean in the context of the new regionalism that has been developing since the 1980s (Rosenthal, 1993; CEPAL, 1994a). As a result, economic integration is seen as 'a series of voluntary decisions by sovereign states to eliminate barriers to trade in goods, services, capital or people' (Smith, 1993, 4). The process of economic integration can be characterised as regional when it develops between sovereign states that share a geographical identity based on the common occupation of land or water. Nevertheless the empirical definition of the geographical areas is based on 'cultural antecedents, social conventions, and political calculations, rather than on impartial intellectual criteria', which can cause possible disputes and even redefinition (ibid.).

Aside from these qualifications and the consequent debate, the regions and the regionalisation process are based on a latent solidarity in the search for a form of collective independence which guarantees a development that is more independent of the world economy. In this sense, regionalisation is often a defence strategy against the outside world, especially against the threats implicit in the formation of other geographically close or contiguous blocs. The process also represents a convergence of interests and a political will to create an expanded market to increase trade, investment and technological transfers. From this perspective a region is conforming to the definition introduced by Deutsch in the 1960s, 'a group of political units with closer links between themselves than with others' (Deutsch, 1969, 95), although this bond is not necessarily limited to the implementation of economic integration. The regional connection can also be founded in collective security agreements, migratory flows, cultural and linguist identity, harmonisation of foreign policies and economic cooperation agreements.

The majority of analysts agree, however, that the component of political will is fundamental, not so much for the construction of regions in formal terms but as the impetus for a regionalisation process that broadens and deepens all the links between the states and societies involved and, in particular, as the impetus for regional integration schemes (Smith, 1993, 2). As a researcher noted recently in relation to the Caribbean Basin, 'in our hemisphere the regions are the product of deliberate political acts, which are continued with stages of intense social and cultural interaction since, to be successful and acceptable, a region must acquire a substance that transcends the terms of its birth certificate' (Giacalone, 1995, 5).

In Latin America and the Caribbean, the proliferation of economic integration schemes and regional free trade agreements is the result of both economic logic and political will. Yet in the Caribbean Basin the convergence of economic logic and political interests is also based on geographical contiguity – however ambiguous and vague that may occasionally appear to be – and on an expression of historical, linguistic and cultural bonds. Examples are the creation of CARICOM and the various forms of Central American integration, including – despite their limitations – political ones such as the Central American Parliament. In spite of the difficulties experienced by these schemes, mainly in the 1970s and 1980s, coupled with the economic and political objectives – and the consequent divergences, tensions and conflicts – outlined here, there are common historical, linguistic and cultural links that form the initial platform for a movement toward regionalisation.

Some authors are convinced that a regionalisation process on the ideological-cultural and symbolic level requires not only the will to overcome the limitations imposed by the traditional concept of national sovereignty in the interests of regional sovereignty, but also the development of a regional nationalism that transcends the local nationalism of the nation state. Hence for the emergence of a regional awareness to support the regionalisation process on the economic and political level, a cultural and historical basis is required which is closely associated with the existence of cultural areas (Smith, 1990, 185–7)[7]. As a result convergence around a regional identity, based on a community of cultural, linguistic and historical traits, is usually an essential though not determinant ingredient for promoting regional initiatives. By using the resource of difference as an element of ideological and regional cohesion, regionalism is in marked contrast to the cultural homogenisation processes generated by globalisation.

For all that, along with the observations already made, the present tendency to form regional blocs often ignores this cultural and historical dimension except for rhetorical references and the difficulties and obstacles that may appear during the regionalisation process (cf. Hurrell, 1992; Mace et al., 1993). Analysis of the regionalisation process in the Caribbean Basin also suffers from this omission despite the fact that the region is characterised by fragmentation and cultural, linguistic, ethnic, religious and political heterogeneity, as well as by economic differences and asymmetries. Despite its colonial genesis this fragmentation and heterogeneity is still a decisive factor in contemporary attempts to redefine the region and in the political fractures and cleavages that occur during the integration process. It may also have a significant effect on the evolution of a regional imaginary – an ideology of regionalisation and a defining and distinct identity as an ideological-cultural and psychological binding for the process.

We will return to this subject shortly noting, in the meantime, that in the Caribbean Basin linguistic and cultural fragmentation is often a major obstacle to the advance of regionalisation. Consequently it must be recognised as a relevant factor in any analysis of Caribbean regionalisation, both in its impetus 'from above' and in its promotion 'from below'. (Serbin, 1987; Serbin and Bryan, 1991; Bryan and Serbin, 1996).

The theoretical debate – between the crisis of paradigms *and theoretical pluralism*

The complexity and rapid change of the contemporary world resulting from globalisation and the release of assimilative and reactive processes are revealing the increasing analytical and interpretative (and even descriptive) limitations of the traditional approaches drawn from the theory of international relations. This trend is caused by the impact of world developments and, as Halliday points out, by the resulting theoretical weaknesses of the study of international relations. It is also affected by the changes and debate in the discipline itself, as well as by the influence of new ideas being developed in other social sciences (Halliday, 1994, 5). For these reasons, it is not sufficient simply to describe the globalisation process and the reactions it generates on the international scene, we must go more deeply, albeit briefly, into the current debate between the competing paradigms, theoretical approaches and perspectives in the field of international relations, and into the supporting epistemological assumptions offered by the social sciences in general.

In its recent development, the discipline of international relations has been characterised, among other things, by low receptivity to contributions from other social disciplines. Despite its association with political theory, the primordial interest of the subject is relations between states as the basis of the international system. Since its emergence at the beginning of this century it has tended to overlook the contributions of political science, sociology, anthropology and, in some of the more dominant approaches, even history and economics. Without going into a detailed discussion of the dominant *perspectives* (Gill and Law, 1988) in international relations, for heuristic purposes, it is useful to make a short critical presentation of the principal arguments and the crisis the discipline is facing in the context of changing global conditions. This brief review will help to develop an appropriate perspective for an analysis of the dynamic of regionalisation in the Caribbean Basin. We will outline the principal theoretical perspectives in the field of international relations in terms of the traditional classification into realism and neorealism, liberal-pluralism and neoliberalism, and globalism, as the three dominant currents. We will then relate this brief review to the three – or according to some authors, four – *debates* in international relations: the first between idealists and realists, the second between traditionalists and behaviourists, and the third between rationalists and reflectivists[8]; and their links with inputs from other disciplines and from inter- and trans-disciplinary approaches.

The approach promoted by the *realist* school emphasises the nation state as a unified, primordial and rational protagonist in the international environment, with recourse to power as *ultima ratio* and to national interest as the only guide for deciphering the intricate dynamic of international relations reduced to a post-Westphalian system of an anarchic and Hobbesian nature (Morgenthau, 1986). This view does not take into account the effect of the domestic political scene on the international dynamic through its impact on the state and political actors in general. It considers the state to be basically an external actor and postulates its condition as a *black box* unaffected by domestic affairs in its exercise of international relations. Similarly this approach tends to ignore the proliferation of actors, spaces and circuits of interaction in the international system (Tomassini, 1989). The realist school was forged in the heat of the *first debate* in the discipline which began in the 1930s in the context of the idealistic conceptions associated with the League of Nations. It prospered with the Cold War, especially in the US[9], since its *policy-oriented* perspective provided a conceptual framework for US policies in the bipolar confrontation with their emphasis on the balance of power and military and political *high politics* to the detriment of social and economic *low politics*.

Starting in the 1970s, *neorealism*, in the *second debate* and under the influence of the quantitative methodological approach of behaviourism and the changes in the international economic system, has gradually incorporated the economic dimension into its conceptual framework, as an increasingly structural view of the international dynamic, without losing its basic assumptions on power and the anarchic nature of the post-Westphalian system of nations, with their Hobbesian inflections[10]. The most prominent representatives of this approach – Hedley Bull and Kenneth Waltz – have stressed the effect of the international structure on the behaviour of states and have further revised realist thought on the primacy of states as actors in the international system and the subordinate role of non-state actors, while recognising the growing importance of international economic relations regulated, from their standpoint, by the states. Even so, despite the correctives, neorealism continues to assume that the political has primacy over the economic. In the last resort this orientation persists in the view that the structure of the global economy is determined by the power of states which is externalised through hegemony (Tooze, 1992, 238).

The alternatives offered by the *neoliberal/pluralist* perspective emphasise the centrality of the dynamic of the market as the fundamental explanation, the importance of non-state actors in the existing international system, the limitations of the state as a unified and rational actor conditioned by the action of domestic forces, and the preoccupation with an international agenda that goes beyond military and political issues to embrace economic and social issues. This approach has proved particularly attractive and is becoming the dominant discourse. Still the view has its limitations since it frequently disassociates the dynamic of the market from the political factors that condition it, by attempting to explain how actors behave outside their sociopolitical and historical context and by promoting an unhistorical and economically reductionist perspective. Conceptually this perspective establishes a clear difference between economics and politics, assigning lesser weight to the latter and a high degree of rationality to the former, particularly in terms of the behaviour of the market economy. Hence, it has influenced the development of a number of variations of what Gill and Law call 'free market conservatism' – studies of public choice which see the determination of national policies, including foreign policy, in terms of supply and demand and the theory of hegemonic stability (Gill and Law, 1988, 46–50).

Over the last twenty years, the controversies between the variations of realism and liberalism have led to the development of a variety of combinations that either accept or question the original presumptions. Particularly controversial is the characterisation of the anarchy of the international system and of power, in the debate between the traditional and the more systematised, quantitative versions of the scientific pretension of behaviourism, which in its extreme positivist tendency has frequently ignored the historical dimension. Although the emphasis and the key concepts stressed by realism and liberalism can differ, particularly in relation to the primacy of political and economic approaches, a dialogue has developed which is influencing both perspectives toward a positivist rationalist orientation that exaggerates the contemporary specificity of phenomena often to the detriment of their historical dimension (Halliday, 1994, 29). As a result, since the 1970s, *neoliberalism*, especially in its institutionalist aspect, has influenced the emergence of variations that focus on *interdependence* (Keohane and Nye, 1988) and the role of cooperative institutions and *international regimes* (Krasner, 1983) for establishing order in the international system. These variations assume that the use of physical coercion is ineffective and highlight the importance of economic cooperation. They also take into account the multiplicity and destructuring of the international agenda and its transnational actors, along with the state's variant role as an international actor under pressure from both the domestic and the international political dynamic.

Strongly marked by the development of the *second debate* on international relations, the *theory of interdependence* is based on three propositions: the loss of the predominant role of the state in international relations in favour of *non-state* forces and actors; dilution of the ranking of international issues in terms of military and political *high politics*, and economic and social *low politics*; and the gradual fading of the importance of military power in international relations (Halliday, 1994, 15). In this context, the theories of interdependence, *foreign policy analysis* and *international political economy* have emerged and developed in the heat of the *second debate*, with a significant impact on the analysis of the transformation of the contemporary international system. In particular, in an effort to view the approaches of the realist school from the perspective of international political economy, Gilpin and others have contributed to the development of the *theory of hegemonic stability*, in relation to the role of the US as world *hegemon* since the decline of the British Empire (Gilpin, 1987).

On the whole this debate has reflected the changes in the international system over the last few decades and their resonance in the specific sphere of the discipline of international relations in the US and the Anglo-Saxon tradition, by assuming a very close association between the solution of practical problems and policy orientation, which is inherent in the pragmatic and utilitarian concept of the rationalist Anglo-Saxon tradition. This situation is a response to the special characteristics of the relationship between the academic world and the political decision makers in the US, evident during the Cold War and in the boom of the realist school[11].

It is useful to qualify the reference to the Anglo-Saxon tradition since the *English school* of international relations, especially its emphasis on *international society* in the work of Wight and his followers, incorporates a more critical and historical view. The attempt to link this latter approach with the logic of structural realism and the theory of international regimes leads to the development of instruments for analysing a complex international society ordered in concentric terms on the basis of diminishing degrees of commitment as the distance from the centre increases, in conditions of unequal development (Buzan, 1993, 327–8)[12]. A significant divergence from this tendency is found in the contributions of Rosenau, briefly commented on earlier, in which he systematises the analysis of global transformations by incorporating concepts such as turbulence and complex change from the theory of chaos (Rosenau, 1990; 1992c)[13].

Perhaps one of the most outstanding elements of these theoretical developments in the field of international relations, in the wake of global transformation and the growing interest in the linkage of political and economic aspects, is the proliferation of theoretical syntheses between the traditional versions of international relations and international political economy, especially evident in the contemporary English school (Gill and Law, 1988; Strange, 1988; McGrew, 1992a; Stubbs and Underhill, 1994a). As a result, the traditional classification of the *second debate* as a confrontation between the traditionalism of realist origins and behaviourism raises serious doubts. One of the consequences seems to be a more open attitude to the linkage between political and economic aspects in the international sphere, and a significant interaction between the concepts of international relations and international political economy. Hence attempts are repeatedly being made to interpret the globalisation process in terms of the structuring of a global economy and its links with a global political world, by development of modalities of cooperation and the establishment of international systems that impose partial focal rules on world anarchy, in an *international order* torn by anarchic competition between its constituent states and the organising forces of the economy.

The *globalist orientations*, among which Wallerstein's contribution (1988) is most relevant, have developed largely at the margin of the Anglo-Saxon academic establishment. This school stresses analysis of the global context with the historical perspective of the development of capitalism, centred on the mechanisms of domination and the asymmetries prevailing in the international system. It has been made more attractive by the incorporation of a structural approach and the inclusion, from the outset, of political economy in its analysis. However, in the analysis of the division between the industrialised North and the developing South – the centre and the periphery, the focus of economic dynamism and the margins of the international system – the danger of being absorbed by another type of economicist approach is disturbing because of its reductionism, particularly in relation to some fashionable *neo-Marxist* perspectives.

The globalist approach assumes a global context and an historical dimension for international relations, emphasising the mechanisms of domination in the development of world capitalism. Following this line of thought, a structural view has developed of the conflict in the international system. In its most extreme versions, the political aspect is a mirror of the economic aspect and the structure of global capitalism, and political institutions, including the state, become an extension of economic relations (Tooze, 1992, 236–7). The structural emphasis is particularly evident in the development of the theory of dependence in the Latin American and African context[14], which views the world as a single economic system dominated by international capitalism. The system is seen as characterised by global economic inequality and unequal exchanges between the centre and the periphery in conditions of exploitation and domination; by the persistent creation of relationships based on dependence between the industrialised North and the developing South; and by the struggle of oppressed peoples against exploitation and domination (Del Arenal, 1990, 15–6). The preoccupation with the dynamic of the system as a whole often diminishes the role of the international actors, in spite of the importance assigned to the role of the social classes in some versions.

A crucial factor in the problem of linking the globalist approaches with the *real* world of international relations lies not so much in their holistic and historical approach, as in the strong structuralist character of their analysis. Although the structures and processes are fully absorbed, the agents that generate the processes and produce changes in the structures are as frequently ignored or relegated to a second plane, as they are by the neorealists (Wendt, 1987). It is significant that as a reaction, some of the more recent contributions in the field of international political economy underscore the political dimension as the basic link between the structures and the agents in specific institutional contexts (Stubbs and Underhill, 1994a, 37).

However, more recent Marxist-inspired versions of the globalist perspective have reclaimed a more dynamic role for social actors in the international system based on a revision of Gramsci's work. This view is related to the linkage of forms of hegemony and counter-hegemony through the formation of transnational alliances and the vanishing of economic determinism since the recovery of the role of culture and ideas (Cox, 1987; Gill, 1993). In this respect, the introduction of the concept of the global civil society is crucial for a full understanding of the globalisation process and its contradictions (Shaw, 1994).

Overall, despite their origins in the intellectual traditions of Western thought and social sciences, the realist/neorealist liberal/pluralist and the globalist approaches are consistent with a rationalist, objective view of world reality, in contrast to a reflectivist orientation which lays the foundations for what is known as the *third debate* in international relations.

The *reflectivist* approach, marked by the post-modern debate in the social sciences (Tomassini, 1991; Rosenau, P., 1992), makes two basic assumptions. Firstly, there is no single rationality or historical narrative that can – on its own terms – provide a complete explanation or make sense of history or any other branch of the social sciences. Secondly, the apparently discrete and unitary categories of the social sciences and other Western forms of interpretation conceal a diversity of meanings and identities which makes political life much more complex and indeterminate than the rationalist approaches might suppose (Halliday, 1994, 37–8). The reflectivist interpretations also adopt some fundamental contributions from a meta-theoretical view of the social sciences – the intertextual character of theory and knowledge in general; the social construction of knowledge in specific historical and social contexts; and the weight of individual experience in the production of this knowledge – as determinants of the different *readings* of world reality (Bierstecker, 1992).

This approach has been particularly fruitful because it has reclaimed the critical contributions of the Frankfurt school – and especially Habermas (Linklater, 1992) – and has introduced a feminist element (Moller Okin, 1991; Weber, 1994) into the social and political conditions in which the narratives of international reality are constructed. It has also incorporated a meta-theoretical and relativist dimension into the discussion on the existing global order. Moreover by relativising the contributions of Western social sciences and their close association with modernity, these post-modern versions have enriched the cognitive horizon of the debate in international relations by incorporating cultural differences and emerging identities into the framework of globalisation. These phenomena, whether of gender as in the case of the feminists, or of cultural diversity in the case of ethnic, national and religious particularisms, challenge the globalisation process as an extreme expression of modern Western rationality.

The variants of the reflectivist approaches (cf. Neufeld, 1993) are a response to the perplexity created by world transformations and to the need to generate a meta-scientific theory based on the criticism of rationalism, positivism and the rational liberal paradigm. They spring from a criticism of modernity in its Western sense; the recovery of subjectivism and irrationality as fundamental assumptions in the generation of knowledge; the revindication of theoretical and conceptual pluralism; and attempts to release *theory* from the rigidity of observation, empirical corroboration and the generalisation of conclusions (Carvajal, 1993, 34). In the more fundamentalist versions of reflectivism, there are doubts about their explanatory capacity and the extent of the knowledge of reality they can produce.

Aside from a meta-theoretical debate (Der Derian and Shapiro, 1989; Walker, 1988), the reflectivists' contribution to the empirical analysis of international reality has been fairly limited. They have, however, generated a proliferation of variegated narratives aimed at deconstructing or breaking down the positivist and rationalist bases of the construction of interpretations in the social sciences and more so in international relations. By calling into question the bases of the construction of interpretations in the social sciences and by criticising the fragmentary assumptions of the division into scientific disciplines, this debate has opened a discussion on the possibility of combining inter-, multi- or trans-disciplinary perspectives in the analysis of international relations, and contemporary world transformations and their complexities. In terms of a revision of the conceptual bases of disciplinary diversity and criticism of Western modernity, this discussion opens the possibility of incorporating a substantive historical view along with contributions from anthropology, sociology and social psychology, especially in relation to the social construction of interpretative schemes, ideological and cognitive frameworks and cultural norms. This could be done by revising the guiding imaginaries in their own contexts using different interlocutors, texts and authors and likewise the narratives used to interpret international reality. The process has also revealed the need to generate new theoretical categories in order to explain the mechanisms of social and symbolic reproduction.

From the field of anthropology, this situation has made possible a revision of the methodological assumptions of the discipline in its historical genesis as the colonial narrative of the 'other' exotic (Augé, 1994a and b). It has also opened the possibility of refounding the discipline from the new perspective of the analysis of international relations in a culturally complex and diverse global world, by radicalising cultural relativism and its postulation of the cultural polyphony of the contemporary world (ibid.). This opening has broadened the conceptual horizon by assimilating significant contributions from social psychology into the analysis of cultural and cognitive differences. As we have dwelt on these contributions and the need for a critical interdisciplinary confluence in other works (Serbin, 1987), we merely mention here that the global transformation processes, in conjunction with the debate begun by post-modernism and the reflectivist approaches, have broadened the discussion on the scope of the interpretation of the international system and the multi- and inter-disciplinary contributions. In addition the meta-theoretical reassessment has opened the way for a revision of international relations with respect to fundamental issues of political science such as the nature of the state, national sovereignty and democracy and in its relationship with sociology, by assigning a global dimension to the analysis of social relations between actors at world level. This has brought about the gradual construction of a sociology of international relations, traditionally silent or absent due to the pre-eminence of relations based on power and economics in the analysis of the international scene (Badie and Smouts, 1992, 145). The inclusion of the dynamic of social actors and civil society and the dilution of the boundaries between the domestic, regional and international spheres in the debate on the globalisation process is crucial.

It is very difficult to opt for a definitive and conclusive perspective in the analysis of international relations in the context of this contemporary debate and the various critical views. However there is the possibility of formulating a multidimensional analysis of global transformations which includes economic and political aspects in a structural approach linked with the role of the agents or actors that have proliferated on the world scene. This introduces a more decisive political dimension and a symbolic cultural aspect – not always reducible to the logic of Western rationality – into the uncertain and turbulent processes of transition. This kind of analysis requires a multifaceted capacity, for combining different approaches and theoretical conceptions, which recognises the complex and dynamic network characteristic of the existing world system. In this respect a large number of analysts are opting for eclectic choices that take the best from each theoretical world (Del Arenal, 1990, 19) and proposing a theoretical pluralism based on the utilisation of different interpretative schemes according to the emphasis or thematic interest of each study.

A similar approach has guided this work. We accept the need for a multidimensional and holistic approach to the interpretation and analysis of a regional agenda that is relevant to the dynamic of international relations in the Caribbean Basin and adapted to all the unordered and frequently overlapping issues. We also accept the use of theoretical perspectives based on the proliferation of issues, actors, agendas, spaces and circuits of interaction. While acknowledging the criticisms of each approach, we use them in this study according to the needs of the subject under consideration. In short, the uncertainty, transitionality and complexity of the international system, and specifically the regionalisation process in the Caribbean Basin, all require a diversified and pluralist approach that provides a flexible, active and complex interpretation of the Caribbean dynamic. The approach must also emphasise the role of the agents and their capacity to influence the system, particularly in the context of the emergence of a transnational civil society.

Ideas, epistemic communities, traditions and state policies

After this review of the conceptual bases and theoretical responses to the ongoing changes in international relations, the remaining questions relate to the third nucleus of problems mentioned in the introduction, 'How can this conceptual and theoretical baggage affect and influence the formulation of specific policies and, in our case, the regionalisation process in the Caribbean Basin?'

In a series of studies and in the debate under way in the discipline of international relations, it is increasingly assumed that ideas can influence foreign policy and international relations – specifically, certain ideas and concepts on the nature of the international system and the impact of globalisation. Goldstein and Keohane categorise ideas in terms of *world views*, *principled beliefs* and *causal beliefs*. In dealing with situations of uncertainty, ideas act as conceptual maps, helping to contend with the absence of simple solutions. They are useful in the design and formulation of strategic initiatives and they can come together to form enduring institutions. Consequently policy changes are influenced by ideas because new ideas emerge and changes take place in conditions which affect the impact of the old ideas. From this point of view ideas are relevant as the outcome of a system of a many interacting causes of which they form part (Goldstein and Keohane, 1993, 29–30). However as the authors themselves recognise, ideas are not produced in a vacuum and they are not separate from interests. The definition of interests implies the existence of beliefs and consequently of ideas (ibid., 26).

But versions that are less rationalist and anchored in more reflectivist views of the sociology of knowledge stress that ideas, and specifically ideology in its more general sense, are produced and reproduced by particular actors in particular historical settings. In this context, ideas and circumstances often reveal a profound and subtle interrelation and interpenetration. As interests are also constructed culturally, an inevitable interpenetration occurs between belief and circumstance, between ideology and immediate situation and, more specifically, between identity and the historical-social context (Hall, 1993, 41–5).

In this respect, in particular social and historical circumstances, certain groups that produce and reproduce ideas, irrespective of any links with their own interests, can become important social actors, especially in situations of crisis, uncertainty and transition, in so far as other actors believe in the veracity of their messages and as long as they have a permanent factual reference. The process of forming an ideological power is historically relevant in the social construction of aspects of reality. This is a basic cultural fact applicable to all social groups, and to the social construction of identities as part of the process of 'imagining communities' described by Anderson (1983).

Moreover the social construction of the identities emerging in conditions of uncertainty may very often even precede the conceptualisation of the interests of the group or imagined community. Accordingly, a *we* has to be defined, usually in contrast to a *they*, before the group's interests can be conceptualised in a more specific way (Hall, 1993, 50–1). The identities formed in this way are complex and, in many cases, multifaceted and superimposed, as shown by some studies on the formation of identities in Latin America and the Caribbean, particularly in their transnational or pan-national dimension (Jácome, 1994; Mato, 1994). Although, under the effect of changing social and historical conditions, these identities are dynamic, they will often respond inertially to longer historical trends and are not always rapidly adaptable to new situations.

Certain groups that formulate and transmit ideas are particularly important in the building of these identities and of the imaginary that defines the boundaries of a community through mechanisms of symbolic communication, interaction and interrelation. In the framework of the globalisation process and the accelerated and complex dynamic of international relations, the construction of transnational identities, like the construction of nationalist or ethnic ideologies, requires the gradual formation of a particular group – the epistemic regional or transnational community – and the creation of specific conditions before it is able to influence international processes and above all policy formulation. Peter Haas (1992) defines *epistemic community* as a network of professionals with a recognised expertise, a demonstrated competence in a particular field and an established authority in an area of political importance in the context of a domain or issue. In this sense, an epistemic community is a set of professionals from different disciplines and formative backgrounds who share (1) a set of normative beliefs and principles which provide a logic for the social action of the members of a community; (2) causal beliefs which stem from their analysis of practices that produce or contribute to a central set of problems in their field, and which can be used as a basis for elucidating the many links between possible policy actions and desired results; (3) notions of validity – inter-subjective criteria, internally defined to evaluate and validate the knowledge in their field of expertise; and (4) a common policy of initiatives – common practices associated with a set of problems to which their professional competence is directed, presumably starting from the conviction that human welfare will be improved as a consequence. In essence, for this author, what unites the members of an epistemic community is a shared belief in the veracity and applicability of certain forms of knowledge or specific truths (Haas, 1992, 5).

In the context of the uncertainty that characterises international relations, the epistemic community is able to provide information and interpretations and to contribute to the creation and maintenance of social institutions that can guide international behaviour. It does so by identifying specific policies for adoption by the nation or the group. This is particularly relevant in the interaction between experts and political decision makers since it can provide the latter with instruments for dealing with the complex situations of uncertainty that characterise the existing international system. Unlike the instruments produced by the bureaucracy these are less malleable under political pressure and adhere more firmly to normative values such as veracity. Because the epistemic community is also conditioned by its social context, group consensus does not necessarily generate truth but rather a consensual knowledge which is less permeable to political pressures and conditioning since it is based on other rules (ibid., 1992, 12). Moreover the conditioning factors associated with the construction of consensual knowledge based on clear rules are less evident in a transnational as opposed to a national framework. Thus the influence of a transnational community can be less affected by immediate political interests and more by the characteristics and values of that community. The existence of a more extended network of diffusion means that the influence of the transnational community may be more sustained and intense than that of national communities (ibid., 15).

However the essence of the problem of the extent of this influence is related to the nature of the contacts between the epistemic community and the political decision makers. These contacts are strongly conditioned by the local political cultures and the inherent models of the relationships between the world of knowledge and the world of political decision makers. The weight of world views historically linked to national political cultures has an impact that is substantially different from the ideas in the field of the formulation and implementation of policies directed at the international scene (Hill and Beshoff, 1994b, 221; Risse-Kappen, 1994, 213–4)[15].

In the field of international relations and, more specifically, of ideas and their influence on the formulation of international policy, the influence of cultural context is particularly relevant, in terms of rules, institutions and mutual receptivity. The dominant model of relations between the national epistemic community and political decision makers in international relations overwhelmingly reflects the US model, among other reasons because of the development of the discipline in that country – as mentioned earlier[16]. The mechanism of interrelation between the academic community and the political decision makers is more fluid, as illustrated by the revolving-door image drawn from the movement between the two worlds. A model of close association between the academic and political worlds has evolved from the combined effect of the division of powers between president and congress; the proliferation of government agencies and congressional committees; and the expansion of competitive lobbies and think-tanks of diverse ideological and political affiliations. Other factors include the traditional availability of funds for research from government agencies and private foundations and a research tradition in the universities, directed toward the development of rational methods for dealing with the problems of government, more in line with the German than the British model. Moreover the liberalism of the dominant political culture in the US is much more open to the image of the expert and to the contribution of rational, scientific analysis to policy (Wallace, 1994, 151).

In this context it is not surprising that the bulk of the output of the discipline of international relations in the US is produced for two interlocutors. The first is the academic community itself because of strongly established consensual mechanisms closely related to the rules for professional careers – particularly *publish or perish* which forces a high degree of academic productivity to ensure job security. The second, mainly from the social sciences and political science in particular, is the political decision makers who require permanent advice and who in turn recruit members of the academic community into their ranks. Consequently the endogenous pressures of the academic world and the exogenous pressures from government and politics generate conditions for a consensual view of the various theoretical approaches. In this framework it is not by chance that the debate in the field of international relations is basically circumscribed to the interrelation of neorealism and liberalism and excludes structural and globalist perspectives, particularly when they are of a Marxist inspiration. Similarly the academic propensity to produce policy-oriented research is not accidental.

Although until the 1950s, Great Britain was, with the US, one of the *two powers* in the development of international relations in the Anglo-Saxon tradition, this relationship has become progressively asymmetric and Great Britain has been left behind in terms of development of the discipline and volume of production[17]. In the relationship between the worlds of academia and of foreign policy decision making, the British model diverges from the US model. In Britain a chasm exists between the two worlds because of what Groom calls the predominance of false mutual images. These distorted perceptions are marked by the search for *truth* in the case of academics and by the association with *power* in the case of the policy makers (Groom, 1988, 192–4). The foreign policy decision makers assume eminently reactive attitudes in dealing with world events and perceive academics in their 'ivory towers' as being particularly ill adapted for grappling with the 'realities' of the international scene. In turn the academics mythologise the capacity for decision making of the bureaucrats and politicians.

In general the chasm between the two worlds is seldom crossed. When it is, it is because the decision makers need specific advice, particularly from the so-called *geographers* or area specialists. This search for advice is not limited to the academic world but often extends to journalists, political party colleagues and interlocutors in general (Hill and Beshoff, 1994b, 215). Furthermore the think-tanks along US lines that proliferated in Britain in the 1980s, developed along more clearly defined ideological and political lines (Wallace, 1994, 149) besides having fewer resources. Even so this model has not led to the parochialisation of international relations in Britain. Firstly, as already mentioned, British academics are more aware of the historical dimension than US academia. Secondly, although the globalist versions of Marxist inspiration have not had an exceptional development, international political economy has flourished in Britain and has had an unusual influence as an integral part of the discipline of international relations[18].

The French model, highly centralised on Paris, is in stark contrast because of the isolation of the world of the political decision makers which has its own centres of production of knowledge and advice. The most notable is the Institut Français des Relations Internationales (IFRI), which has tended to side-step the sensitive issues of French foreign policy. A broader and more critical view is offered by the researchers of the Centre d'Etudes pour les Relations Internationales (CERI), the Centre Nationale pour la Recherche Scientifique (CNRS) and researchers in the universities (Wallace, 1994, 154). These institutes frequently adopt theoretical structuralist approaches (under the influence of Claude Levi-Strauss) and globalist approaches that emphasise the cultural dimension of international relations, in a French tradition related to the *francophonie* (cf. Badie and Smouts, 1992).

Finally the Soviet model, while it lasted in its centralised form with state control of domestic structures, generated its own pattern of interrelation which subordinated the academic community to the decisions of state and party. But in the 1980s the possibility opened up for institutions such as the Institute of World Economy and International Relations to produce alternative, even critical, approaches (Wallace, 1994, 156).

Discussion of these different political and intellectual traditions is justified because their models have influenced the relationship between the academic world and political decision makers in Latin America and the Caribbean and because they illustrate the extent of the influence of ideas on policy formulation in the region[19].

Unfortunately there are no studies on relations between academia and the political decision makers in international relations in Latin America and the Caribbean. We have nothing more than a few studies that indirectly refer to the influence of certain ideas and theoretical approaches on foreign policy (Van Klaveren, 1984; Van Klaveren, 1992; Russell, 1992). The studies agree on the influence of legal and geopolitical traditions in terms of the involvement of the legal profession and the military in the analysis of international relations and in the early stages of foreign policy formulation in Latin American countries. This kind of involvement is characteristic of Latin American political systems with their highly centralised political cultures which in this century have steered a narrow course between the rule of law and the authoritarianism of de facto governments.

In spite of efforts to return to realist interpretations in the analysis of international relations from the 1960s to the 1980s, the dependence-oriented approaches have exerted a strong globalist influence from the perspective of international political economy. These approaches were stimulated by ECLAC's analysis of centre-periphery relations, by more orthodox versions inspired by the Marxist theory of imperialism and by the qualified approaches that emerged later in Brazil and Chile (Van Klaveren, 1992, 186–7). The degree to which the Latin American elite absorbed these views is illustrated by the implementation of the strategy of import substitution for more than two decades in the majority of Latin American countries. It is very difficult, however, to make a complete evaluation of the permeability of the elite to these views because of the absence of specific studies.

In the English-speaking Caribbean, a similar line has been followed – more slowly and linked to theoretical developments in Africa – by the New World Group and by some radically Marxist variants, among a second generation of academics and intellectuals closely associated with the post-colonial phase in these countries (Serbin, 1987; Sankatsing, 1994). Once again the absence of systematic research on the subject makes an effective evaluation of their relationship with the world of political decision makers very difficult. Also in the English-speaking Caribbean, the Institute of International

Relations of the University of the West Indies, since its creation in the 1970s, has trained many members of the region's diplomatic corps, but their postgraduate studies in Great Britain and the US seem to have had more effect on the diplomats and decision makers of the English-speaking Caribbean countries. In short, despite the spread of ideas from the academic community to the political decision makers who tend to be influenced by the dependentist ideas of the New World Group related to ECLAC, the impression is that there has been no systematic contact between the two worlds, neither in Latin America nor in the Caribbean, with the exception of special cases such as Mexico.

This situation may result from the absence of models of linkage and tradition but an hypothesis that cannot be ruled out is the absence of a critical mass of academic resources. The demands of academic life in Latin America and the Caribbean with its low pay, heavy teaching and administrative load and lack of financial resources, have hindered the development of pragmatic research aimed at influencing policies or providing knowledge and information to political decision makers. In addition, the traditional alter-centrism or dependence syndrome means that decision makers place more value on the advice or expertise offered by consultants or academics from the United States and Great Britain.

Although these general statements are valid, the intellectual traditions in each of the linguistic and cultural areas of the Caribbean Basin do create specific models of interrelation between the world of academics and intellectuals and the world of the political and bureaucratic decision makers. This explains the contrast in the Spanish-speaking areas between the customary compartmentalisation of the two worlds in Central America, Colombia and Venezuela, and the influence of statist or liberal models with greater contact but with differentiated features in Mexico, Cuba and Puerto Rico. The contrast is also apparent in the English-speaking Caribbean with the persistence of the British model and in the French-speaking Caribbean – mainly the Overseas Departments of Guadeloupe, Martinique and Guiana – influenced by the French model. In the Dutch-speaking Caribbean the link is absent in Aruba and the Netherlands Antilles probably due to the low level of academic development and in Suriname because of political turbulence. Obviously in the latter case and in the English-speaking Eastern Caribbean, the smallness of the societies and the absence of a critical mass makes consideration of specific models very difficult since most of the human resources available are recruited into the political world and the state bureaucracy with no independently-developed academic sphere.

Maps for navigation

The analysis that follows is based on a series of specific theoretical-conceptual premises that take in and synthesise some of the discussions of the preceding pages in order to sketch a conceptual *map for navigation* through the remainder of the book.

First, the analysis assumes that the existing dynamic of the international economic system tends to dilute the boundaries between the international and the domestic, generating a series of *intermestic* processes based on their linkage in the regionalisation process. According to Salvador Arriola, this process (or mega-trend) 'relates to the loss of importance of national borders due to the transnationalisation of trade, capital and technology flows. The state is no longer the only actor, and the international organisations (or the normal mechanisms of economic negotiation) have been overtaken by a reality in which other actors not connected with governments and national interests intervene more rapidly and effectively' (Arriola, 1995, 90–1).

Second, despite the trend toward 'globalisation' of thought based on giving priority to the linkage of global and domestic dynamics, the analysis assumes that these processes generate a specific dynamic that is expressed in a regionalisation process which is characterised by conditions of complex interdependence in terms of geographical, cultural and political conditionings. This takes the form of an asymmetric and unequal interdependence between the dual nuclei of the commercial and financial dynamic and of information and technological innovation on the one hand, and a periphery threatened by marginalisation from the international political economy on the other. In this sense globalisation is not an homogenisation of the international economic system but a deepening of the inequality between states, regions and non-state actors (Hurrell and Wood, 1995, 468).

Third, the conjunction of globalising trends with regional processes produces a specific dynamic which, like the global, is not limited to intergovernmental relations but takes in a broad spectrum of transnational interactions and processes between an increasingly complex and diffuse set of actors. This process does not produce homogenisation and standardisation of regional interactions since the regional dynamic, by refracting and sifting the global dynamic, generates substantially different local situations (Stallings, 1995, 22).

Fourth the analysis of any regionalisation process must involve an increasingly complex set of actors which transcends exclusively governmental action and creates a web of conflicting interests, strategic alliances and consensus built on cooperation and institutionalisation, but which continues to nurture the fragmentation and cleavage inherent in the regional dynamic. However due weight is given to the state's key role in the international dynamic, although increasingly conditioned and pressured by other actors and elements, and to the role of the emerging transnational civil society (Shaw, 1994).

Finally the analysis presupposes that the interaction of these actors is focused not only on economic processes but more particularly on political and ideological-cultural processes and on a series of specific socio-political effects, where the values and normative presumptions – be they implicit or explicit – determine the discursive logic and the highly complex specific actions that affect the international and regional dynamic at different levels.

In this respect, the harmonisation of the dominant economic ideology at global level has been structured around a consensual discourse of three elements – macroeconomics stability; a reduced role for government in the economy (deregulation and privatisation); and a more extensive opening to the outside world through the dismantling of trade barriers and an attractive climate for foreign investment (Stallings, 1995, 12). However in the early 1990s this consensus began to break down in the nuclei of economic dynamism and the multilateral financial agencies, as well as progressively on the periphery, due to the need for an integrated approach to the macro-economics objectives and social imbalances that these economic policies generate (SELA, 1995).

In view of the fractures in this consensus and the focus on the social effects of policies, it is assumed that all regionalisation processes, initially based on cooperation as a first step toward regional integration, require the involvement and participation of the traditional actors – governments acting in their national interests – along with an increasingly complex network of social, political, economic, cultural actors with transnational projection, on the understanding that *regionalisation from above* is necessarily linked to *regionalisation from below*. Due to the limited availability of expert human resources, this situation requires a strengthened regional epistemic community capable of providing specialised knowledge and expert advice to the political decision makers. The central element of the regionalisation process should be an effort to promote, in the neofunctionalist sense, closer contacts between the political and governmental elite and the private sector, as well as with intellectuals and academics, and non-governmental organisations.

The growth of the actors involved in the transnational and in this case regional, dynamic also generates a proliferation of narratives, approaches, interpretations and discourses as individual interpretations of regional developments, although maintaining as reference the dominant economic discourse. This proliferation of narratives and discourses amplifies and diversifies the spectrum of identities and projects which in turn deepens fragmentation in a region that is already heterogeneous and varied.

Based on these premises and faced with an heteroclitic mosaic of fragmented and divided identities, multiple and contradictory discourses, individual narratives and interpretations – despite the atmosphere of uniformity, the first question that comes to mind on the region is, 'Which Caribbean are we talking about?' Definitions and conceptualisations abound in direct proportion to the discourses and narratives that proliferate and nourish the different identities. Yet none of them can be disregarded and all respond, to some extent, to the characteristics of the historical-social and political framework in which they are generated and to the actors that formulate them under the pressure of political, ideological and linguistic circumstances and individual biographical processes.

Notes

1 Based on a paper originally presented at the XIX Convention of the Latin American Studies Association (LASA), held in Washington in September 1995, under the title *Theories, paradigms, approaches and perspectives in the study of the contemporary Caribbean*.
2 Compare for example, the analysis of the role of multinational corporations and the stimulus of consumerism in the process of globalisation in Sklair (1991).
3 As the introduction to this volume states in more detail: 'Globalization from below, in contrast to globalization from above, aims to restore to communities the power to nurture their environments; to enhance the access of ordinary people to the resources they need; to democratize local, national, and transnational political institutions; and to impose pacification on conflicting power centers'. (Brecher et al., 1993, xv).
4 Some analyses would extend this triad to a future quintet – the US, the European Union, Japan, the newly-industrialised Asian countries (NICs) and the members of ASEAN, and China (SELA, 1993, 65).
5 With reference to regional subsystems of security, some analysts believe that it is very difficult to establish their geographical boundaries and even their functional boundaries.
6 Smith adds, 'Integration thus provides information, establishes common expectations, and assures a level of predictability. Intergovernmental co-operation, on the other hand, results from ad hoc bargaining between sovereign states; it does not

Perplexities and uncertainties in the global world 31

necessarily occur within a framework of long-term expectations, convergent interests, and shared benefits. To put it another way, regional integration can facilitate intergovernmental co-operation among member states, but intergovernmental co-operation can (and usually does) occur in the absence of regional integration schemes' (Smith, 1993, 5).

7   The stumbling blocks, in the two processes of subregional integration mentioned, are not obstacles to recognising the importance of this ideological-cultural base.

8   Halliday considers that the third debate was the result of the introduction of structuralism and Marxism into international relations, and that the debate between rationalists and reflectivists is in fact a *fourth debate* (Halliday, 1994, 37).

9   The pre-eminence that this approach acquires in the Anglo-Saxon, especially the North American context, and the consequent development of international relations in the academic world of the US, justifies in this sense Stanley Hoffman's statement that 'international relations is a North American science' (Hoffman, 1988).

10 With respect to this debate, in addition to Keohane's classic compilation (1986), compare the introductory chapter of Baldwin (1993). For a more recent view of the scope of this debate in the theory of international relations, see Powell's review (1994).

11 It is no coincidence that in one of the academic temples of the US – the University of Harvard – political science is institutionally inserted into the departments and schools under the heading Government.

12 For a view of the changes in the model of relations between the academic world and the world of decision making in international policy in the British sphere see Hill and Beshoff (1994a).

13 For a discussion of the contributions to this theory, see Sametband (1994) and, in a popular version, Gleick (1987).

14 In the Caribbean, with the necessary qualifications, this perspective can be identified in the contributions made in the 1970s by the New World Group, compare in this respect Serbin (1987) and Sankatsing (1994).

15 From this perspective the author adds that in the field of international studies, 'structural theories of international relations need to be complemented by approaches that integrate domestic politics, transnational relations, and the role of ideas if we want to understand the recent sea change in world politics' (Risse-Kappen, 1994, 213). On the ideas he emphasises that the political culture as part of the domestic structure 'contains only those ideas that do not change often and about which there is societal consensus' (ibid., 209).

16 As Olson and Groom point out, 'The United States is pre-eminent in the quantity of research produced; many of the leaders of the field from all over the world have found succour in North American universities – a particularly perverse form of "brain drain," ' which, as the authors themselves remark, has possibly tended to make the field more insular (Olson and Groom, 1991, 325).

17 As Olson and Groom add, after the golden age, 'for the most part, it was a matter of getting on the American bandwagon or getting nowhere' (Olson and Groom, 1991, 139).

18 'In the United States, the legal tradition in International Relations to some extent blocked the growth of International Political Economy, until political scientists became fascinated by the emergence of European economic integration and formulated the theory of neofunctionalism ... International Political Economy has thus flourished in Britain as an organic part of International Relations' (Olson and Groom, 1991, 297). Compare Tooze (1994) for a further discussion of the

development of international political economy. For a more detailed analysis of relations between academics and political decision makers in Great Britain, see the collective work edited by Hill and Beshoff (1994a).
19 We have disregarded the cases of Germany and Japan because of their negligible influence on the Caribbean.

2 | Crisis of identity and reconfiguration of the Caribbean Basin[1]

'A certain rhythm and a certain way of being'
Antonio Benitez Rojo

The building of regional identities

Until very recently the Caribbean Basin and the insular Caribbean were identified and categorised predominantly from outside. The Caribbean, the Antilles, the West Indies or the Caribbean Basin were distinct regions originally born out of the metropolitan imaginary – first European and later North American. As in the Borges' story, the Caribbean, in its different versions, begins by being dreamed by *others*, from the chimera of El Dorado for the European *conquistadores* to the tropical paradise of modern tourists, by way of buccaneers' and privateers' dreams of riches in the context of the intra-European conflicts that plagued the region until the ideological mirages of the Cold War (Borges, 1974, 451–5).

In this genesis from outside, the region was categorised as the exotic 'other', whether as seducer or as threat; the external 'other', whose differences were strategically, economically and sexually attractive, and which threatened the identity of the coloniser. In this context the region was born out of difference – out of the contrasting ideology of the *other* – as the object that never becomes subject, whose identity was constructed from outside on the prejudices and assumptions of those who defined it. The search for its own endogenous identity clashed with this original genesis, which was generally disqualifying or, at least, deceptive.

The attempts to establish an identity from within had to contend with the difficulties inherent in any construction of identity, mainly the need for differentiation from the *other* which imposed its own definition from outside, as well as a need for contrast. Another difficulty was the relationship with the formation of the nation state, which involved negative exclusionary practice related to a perceived threat or danger to the shaping of a common identity or nationality. In this process, primarily in the first stages of decolonisation and post-colonial consolidation, the elite of the region's emerging states imitated the formation of the metropolitan identity. Moreover, the colonial legacy of fragmentation hindered the construction of a wider identity than the insular – an identity which embraced the entire region – by limiting and constricting efforts at nativisation or endogenisation. Parochial identities emerged, while the metropolitan *other* was mythicised and the geographical, cultural and ethnic differences of the neighbour disqualified.

Gradually, however, the metropolitan *other* became diffused and ambiguous. The threat was not clearly defined and rather than looking to the external *other* for references for differentiation, it was the differences and contrasts of the neighbour which were seen as a threat to identity because of linguistic, cultural, ethnic and colour differences. Historically, therefore, in the Caribbean there is no common identity built around the myth of a shared culture or a communality of values in the presence of an external threat; no re-creation of the region's own *imaginary community*. What proliferates are partial, fragmentary identities that create the region's polyphony and heterogeneity but also multiply the *Caribbeans* – the Afro-Saxon, Latin, Hispanic, Afro-Latin, mestizo, English-speaking, insular or continental since there is no common generating myth that creates a unifying identity.

In most cases, the region's geographical insularity does nothing to counteract this fragmentation. On the contrary, the geography of the region tends to reinforce the colonial legacy of cleavage and division. As Colin Clarke remarks of the islands, 'Insularity so fragments the Caribbean that its 30 million inhabitants are divided among fifty societies. Social and political boundaries coincide with islands. Only Hispaniola, divided between Haiti and the Dominican Republic, and St Martin, partitioned by France and the Netherlands – are shared by two polities. Each island is clearly bounded by living space, isolated from neighbours by the sea' (Clarke, 1985, 122). Added to this situation are the differences between the English-, Spanish-, Dutch- and French-speaking islands; the Central American countries and Belize; the continental Spanish-speaking countries and the British, Dutch and French Guianas.

Moreover, the identities emerging out of the colonial legacy and the dominant insularity not only strengthen regional fragmentation but cling to static, essentialist views, in their hegemonic or dominant discourses and their underlying logic, without discontinuities or historical changes. We have analysed in another work, the changes of identity in the English-speaking Caribbean in terms of the decolonisation process and the evolution from an Anglo-Saxon to an Afro-Caribbean identity.

We noted then that the effort invested in the process of building a fragile, partial and incipient identity brings with it a disposition to settle for anachronistic myths in which the impact of change and transformation is absent, and an essential timelessness is assumed (Serbin, 1989b). For this reason the identities tend to be historically fixed and anchored in their own isolation, without assuming the discontinuities and the dynamic imposed by a changing reality. They maintain the categorisations and stereotypes that emerged with the original identifying myth. This is shown in a very radical way by the official discourses which continue to emphasise, with nuances, the myths of anti-colonialism or racial differences. Consequently, the construction of a regional identity is held back by, among other things, the absence of actors, institutions and ideologies with a broad, dynamic perspective capable of overcoming parochial and insular discourses and reductionist legacies (Boxill, 1993).

As we have mentioned, the political elite that lead the decolonisation processes have frequently had to reinforce these parochial and reductionist discourses, in the interests of constructing an anti-colonial, and identifying, national ideology for the emerging nation state. They have done this as a means of differentiating themselves from the metropolis and reaffirming the distinct identity of the emerging nation states. This is just as valid for the countries of the continental area, or the Central American isthmus, as it is for the insular states that gained their independence at a later date. Within this context, apart from the economic and political obstacles facing the integration process in the region, one of the greatest difficulties is the incapacity to overcome these discourses by articulating a language of regional communality which goes beyond the identification of the *other*, differentiated as a threat and consequently defined in negative and exclusionary terms. This discourse could create a vision of a flexible communality open to change and based on common values, characteristics and problems. There are, in fact, insistent historical, psychological and cultural obstacles in the way of 'imagining a new community', to paraphrase Anderson (1983).

For this reason, what is now required is a founding ideology, that anchors regional communality with an open, creative and shared vision of the region and its destiny, able to meet the challenge from the more specific threat of marginalisation from the international system. Two things are required to develop this vision; firstly the capacity to overcome the restricted views of nationality, sovereignty and identity promoted by the political elite that are traditionally associated with the emergence of the nation state; secondly the formulation of an innovative *imaginary* and project shared by regional civil society and by the myriad of actors committed to the region. This is perhaps the greatest challenge facing the integration process in the region and the institutional channels emerging around it. Any new identity for the region, in response to external pressures, requires a vision that emphasises common features and values without abandoning differences and heterogeneities. Perhaps the binding elements of the Caribbean Sea itself and the endogenous and exogenous threats faced by the region, with their individual nuances and differences, could be the first steps in the construction of this imaginary. In this respect, the preamble of the Constitutive Agreement of the Association of Caribbean States is particularly explicit: 'Recognising the importance of the Caribbean Sea as a common asset of the peoples of the Caribbean, the role it has played in its history and its potential for operating as a unifying element in its development' (ACS, 1994b, 3).

The building of a regional consensus around common, unifying values requires the creation of a regional imaginary based on the identification of common interests and values as part of a vision backed by a firm political will. It also depends on institutions that anchor the shared regional vision to the active participation of the social and political actors involved. This participation must involve a very diverse set of actors, with different agendas, whose interests are not always compatible with those of the elite, which are primarily concerned with regionalisation initiatives. Appropriate participative mechanisms have to be created and existing mechanisms broadened in an effort to build consensus, if progress is to be made towards regional integration in a democratic and participative framework.

Contemporary genealogy of the Caribbean Basin

We have analysed, in other works, the definitions that gave rise to the identification of the Caribbean Basin as a distinctive region of the hemisphere, differentiated from Latin America (Serbin, 1989a and 1990). What interests us here is the linkage between specific international dynamics in different historical situations and the formulation of regional definitions, from the perspective of the state actors involved and based on different agendas, priorities and interests. The important aspect of this linkage is the historical conditioning that the international and hemispheric systems have imposed on the regional dynamic.

Although the debate on the different conceptualisations of the region can be traced back almost to the 15th century with the arrival of Christopher Columbus in the *New World*, the term Caribbean, 'as the name of a geographical region is a 20th century invention', in the context of the transition in the region from European colonialism to the hegemony of the US (Gaztambide-Géigel, 1995, 2). In fact it emerged as a term for the region at the end of the 19th century and took on increasing relevance, particularly in the US where it was frequently confused with the rest of Latin America at perceptual and political level[2].

Despite its ambiguity, this perception, frequently tinged with ethnocentrism and prejudice, has oriented many of the assumptions underlying US hemispheric policy in this century. The geopolitical view from Washington was not always disassociated from the not-so-implicit racial concepts linked to the 'white man's burden' and 'manifest destiny' (Horsman, 1985; Maingot, 1994a). However, the dimensions that have weighed most heavily in this *narrative* and the actions it has justified, fundamentally relate to the geopolitical sphere. As Maingot notes, if one word had to be chosen to encapsulate the history of the Caribbean, it would be 'geopolitics', in its combination of geography with international relations (Maingot, 1994a, 1).

Yet, recent history shows that, rather than a single 'Caribbean', there are many 'Caribbeans' because the definitions of the region serve their own purposes (Knight and Palmer, 1989, 3), to the point where analysts have no hesitation in referring to a 'geopolitical' Caribbean; an 'ethno-historical' Caribbean; an 'economic' region; or to a cultural area identified with Afro-Central America and with the plantation economy (Gaztambide-Géigel, 1995, 23). In short there is a multitude of regional narratives that illustrate its heterogeneity, multiplicity and plasticity, and whose essence was captured by Benitez Rojo in more postmodern terms in his version of the region 'as a certain rhythm, and a certain way of being' (Benitez Rojo, 1989).

It is only possible to synthesise some of the more recent conceptualisations, in terms of specific situations and actors with their variegated interests and objectives, while accepting the frequently transitory and obsolescent historicity of the many definitions of the region. After the Second World War the region was identified with a series of international situations, on the basis of three fundamental definitions that have occupied first place in the conceptualisation of the region since the 1960s, namely geostrategic, ethno-historic, and Third World definitions.

The *geostrategic* definition of the *Caribbean Basin* materialised during the bipolar confrontation that characterised the Cold War particularly in the aftermath of the triumph of the Cuban revolution, the decolonisation processes in the non-Hispanic Caribbean and, later on, the outbreak of the Central American crisis. This view is in line with the security interests of the US in the region and took shape in the 1980s with the formulation of the Caribbean Basin Initiative (CBI) focused on the insular and Central American countries that met its requirements – especially not to be associated with the socialist camp. This perspective, clearly identified with the assumptions of *realpolitik* and the realist paradigm in international relations, prioritised, in pursuance of US interests, the strategic-military containment of Cuban-Soviet influence as the defining element in the region without necessarily creating a unitary and rigid conceptualisation.

Since the 1980s some US analysts have assumed a wider definition that embraces three concentric circles – the English-speaking Caribbean; the Caribbean archipelago including all the islands, Belize and the three Guianas; and the Caribbean Basin including the nations of Central America and the South American coast (Erisman and Martz, 1982, ix). Despite the flexibility of this definition which sometimes excluded or included Colombia, Mexico and Venezuela but which forced geography to include El Salvador as part of the Caribbean Basin, the conceptualisation assumed the orientation imposed by Washington during the Cold War and in its political materialisation in the Caribbean Basin Initiative[3] (Grupo de Trabajo del Consejo Atlántico, 1985, 13–65).

In this perspective, the North American historical perception of its security interests in the region was defined by three objectives, 'a) establish and maintain a safe, stable and friendly southern peaceful flank; b) guarantee U.S. access to raw materials, trade, opportunities for investment and transport routes in the area; and c) keep hostile powers out' (Child, 1985, 146) which became particularly clear during the Cold War. From this standpoint the differences, between an area such as Central America – defined by common historical, linguistic and cultural experiences – and the insular fragmentation of the Caribbean with its diversity of legacies and divisions, were subsumed by the dominant strategic orientation.

The *ethno-historic* definition emphasises the identification of the *West Indies* with the process of decolonisation and post-colonial consolidation of the non-Hispanic Caribbean. It underscores the common historical experience moulded by the plantation economy, slavery and the incorporation of population contingents from Africa into the insular societies of the Caribbean Sea, the Guianas and Belize. This conceptualisation not only marks out differences with the former European metropolises and the US, but also with the continental neighbours of Latin America. It prioritises the ethno-historical identity of the regional societies and emphasises the capacity for convergence of the collective regional interests that reaffirm the independence and self determination of states in the post-colonial consolidation phase.

This definition has been consistently used by the politicians and analysts of CARICOM's English-speaking member states – especially in formal discourses, in reports and studies by its consultants and analysts, and in the work of researchers from the three campuses of the University of the West Indies and other academic centres in the Anglophone Caribbean. It was favoured in the 1970s by the historian and prime minister of Trinidad, Sir Eric Williams, particularly during the tensions between his country and Venezuela. It also fuelled until very recently the bulk of the rhetoric of the English-speaking Caribbean (with a remarkable conciliatory recognition of Cuba, Puerto Rico and Haiti) and its political and social scientists, with strong resonance among specialists and diplomats from Great Britain. Yet, this conceptualisation was frequently contrasted with a reticence to embrace a broader regional awareness, and overcome insular barriers. The weight of the colonial legacy and insular fragmentation made 'West Indian consciousness' into an exceptional and limited phenomenon (Clarke, 1985, 132)[4].

The third definition views the Caribbean Basin from the standpoint of political economy and is often seen as a *Third World view* – in the context of efforts by developing countries to promote a New World Economic Order (NWEO) in the 1970s. It emphasises the community of interests and priorities of developing countries and the South in general in their relations with the industrialised countries of the North and the possibilities for South-South cooperation. In this view the Caribbean includes the Antillean insular countries, the Central American countries and the *regional powers* of the 1970s, among them Cuba, Mexico, Venezuela and Colombia. Probably the best illustration of this conceptualisation was the one behind the founding of the Latin American Economic System (SELA) in 1975 with the participation of several Anglophone Caribbean countries and the rest of South America – the US being explicitly excluded. From the point of view of political economy, the priorities were for regional convergence on the need for the socio-economic development of the peripheral countries, in a context of asymmetric – if not dependent – relations with the industrialised countries. With inflections strongly influenced by ECLAC, this definition fed the rhetoric of many politicians and not a few analysts and consultants, who did include, however, a substantial component of political economy into their analysis.

Along with defining a specific geographical space, each of these conceptualisations has stressed, in tune with their different focuses, the cleavages and fragmentation of the region, beyond the colonial legacies of the European metropolises and the linguistic division between the Spanish-, English-, Dutch- and French-speaking Caribbeans.

For the *geostrategic* conceptualisation the division of the Caribbean Basin was clearly based on the confrontation between Soviet and Western blocs, making Cuba the focus of Soviet expansion in the region, particularly as allied or sympathetic governments emerged in Nicaragua, Grenada, Suriname, Jamaica and Guyana in the 1970s (cf. Serbin, 1989a). The *other* was identified with the Cuban-Soviet threat and the ideological and political differences in the region. They had to be contained and eliminated as germs that were endangering political stability and US interests in the Caribbean Basin, in clear accord with the assumptions of the realist perspective in international relations. For the *ethno-historic* conceptualisation the region was divided between the English-speaking independent states of the Caribbean and the Spanish-speaking states of the Basin, each with its distinctive historical matrixes, colonial legacies and racial composition. The contrasting and differentiated *other* was identified with the distinctive ethnic and cultural components of Latin America, often perceived through the colonial prejudices still existing in the region. The framework for this definition was a non-Hispanic West Indies, culturally and linguistically closer to its former European metropolises and differentiated from an Hispanic Caribbean linked to Latin America. Finally, from the *Third World* point of view the cleavage in the region was associated with the tensions and asymmetries in relations between developed and developing countries where the *other* was identified with the industrialised North, under the influence of the assumptions implicit in the ECLAC-influenced concepts of the theory of dependence.

Aside from the obvious way in which these perceptions tinged the assumptions underlying regional and extra-regional initiatives, they were also frequently woven into the discourses of the political and economic elite, deepening and complicating cleavage and fragmentation in the region.

Narratives, readings and reinterpretations

These definitions and their resulting identities linked the imaginary, ideologies and narratives of the political elite of the states – and some intellectuals – with frequent references to a logic of the state and influenced the formulation and implementation of specific foreign policies by state actors. These policies were based on particular concepts of national interest and sovereignty, influenced by a range of nationalist components – from the *manifest destiny* of some, to the ethnic identification and the national self determination of others. As a result, in the international situations that affected the region from the 1950s onwards, policies favoured the role of the regional and extra-regional states, their governments and their different perceptions of national interest[5]. The perspective of the international system was eminently *realist*, defined by the dynamic of interstate relations, national interest and the regional and international balance of power.

Thus the essential element of the dominant definition of the Caribbean Basin was the prioritisation of strategic security issues in line with the national interest of the US. By contrast, the other definitions favoured the self determination and independence of the region's states, putting more emphasis on the economic-political or cultural dimension based on a reaffirmation of national sovereignties belatedly developed in the post-colonial phase (Serbin, 1987). This latter *perspective* was often assumed, by sectors of the regional and extra-regional economic and business elite, in terms of the identification of national and regional markets for trade and investment circumscribed by national and subregional regulations, particularly in the Caribbean Basin Initiative (CBI). This was part of a progressive shift away from more orthodox realist views linked to security issues toward neorealist and liberal/pluralist perspectives with more emphasis on economic issues. Globalist and neoMarxist assumptions were relegated to academic sectors and networks and increasingly to some non-governmental organisations and social movements in the region. These questioned the prevailing dynamic, particularly the ideas that inspired structural adjustment, liberalisation and economic opening, and integration under the influence of a pragmatic orientation.

This brief *genealogy* of the prevailing regional identities and the narratives and references that underpinned them until the 1980s, with their individual transitory characteristics and their specific variations and qualifications, is now having to contend with the new global, hemispheric and regional conditions that began to take shape in the 1990s after the dissolution and collapse of the communist bloc and the end of the Cold War. These new conditions provoked an *identity crisis* in the Caribbean and the change and proliferation of perceptions and narratives of its characterisation and identification.

Since the 1980s with the outbreak of the foreign debt crisis in the region and developing countries in general, coupled with the dilution of the strategic priorities brought about by the end of bipolarity, the international situation has been shaped by processes that are increasingly linked to the dynamic of the global political economy (Stubbs and Underhill, 1994a; Gill and Law, 1988; Gilpin, 1987; Tomassini, 1991), and which have resulted in the spread of trends that are now having a significant impact on the complex network of economic, political, cultural and social factors in the region. These processes, which we will discuss in more detail in later chapters, emphasise the need to promote different modalities of intra-regional economic co-operation, based on free trade agreements, subregional integration schemes and functional policies of cooperation between the countries of the region. In this context a *wider* vision[6] of the region is gradually emerging, identified as the *Greater Caribbean*. This vision groups the insular states and territories with the Central American and continental countries from a perspective that partially rescues some of the elements of the Third World conceptualisation, with its emphasis on political economy as the defining paradigm. It also recovers a view of the Caribbean Basin as an area identifiable by the communality of its problems and challenges in the context of the globalisation and regionalisation processes.

The creation of the Association of Caribbean States in 1994 is the materialisation of this idea. It seeks to reduce the inertial effects of the Cold War, colonial legacies, ethnic differences and economic asymmetries by forging a new vision of a region that is in the throes of reconfiguration, and of the Caribbean Sea as *the shared regional heritage* and the basis for a convergence of interests. Yet, this new conceptualisation is plagued by the problems and obstacles created by its original multifaceted genealogy, the demands imposed on it by globalisation and the difficulties standing in the way of its future development in a changing world. Apart from some apparent certainties, the result is a clear *identity crisis* in a changing environment of modified expectations.

Toward the Greater Caribbean as a new founding myth?

From this general perspective of the impact of the global, regional and national transformations on the Greater Caribbean, the original question on its definition and its future existence as an explicitly differentiated region resurface. Some analysts reformulate the question in more negative terms by asking why the region is so divided and unable to move its integration process forward (Dominguez, 1993, 11). For others the question centres on the viability of the Caribbean as a 'functional' and 'coherent' region able to benefit from an integration that goes deeper than a common interest in regional trade and security (Kaiser, 1994, 37). Some authors reduce these questions to a view of the region circumscribed to the English-speaking or insular Caribbean. Others, in this context or in a wider one, attribute some inherent identifying quality to the region, which transcends historical changes and creates a distinctive regional essence.

Aside from the proliferation of views and perspectives of the region, a social imaginary has appeared in recent years with a central symbolic reference – the debate on regionalism and regional integration in the Greater Caribbean and the recent advances along that road. As pointed out by the CARICOM Secretary General in relation to the creation of the ACS 'the initiative of forging an Association of Caribbean States, which includes both the islands and territories of the Caribbean Sea as well as the countries of Central and South America with Caribbean coastlines, setting aside the linguistic differences and the historically underlying imperial affinities, represents a great challenge in contemporary history. Especially for those who consider the Caribbean Sea not as a separatist force, but as a common heritage, which unites all the participating units' (Carrington, 1994, 1).

In this context regionalism in the Greater Caribbean is fundamentally a reaction to external and domestic challenges that require the collective response of 'building a regional community' (Whiting, 1993, 42; Mols, 1993, 51). This response basically involves the identification of shared values, common purposes and a regional identity (ibid., 18), in a wider geographical context than the strictly insular, which presages the gradual vanishing of insular parochialism. This regional identification is restricted to three dimensions – a common historical experience and a common problem; the existence of socio-cultural, political and or economic links; and the development of subregional organisations.

In the first dimension the societies of a specific geographical area have a common historical experience and face the same problem (Stubbs and Underhill, 1994c, 331). In the instance of the Greater Caribbean this common experience relates to its genealogy as an ever wider geopolitical unit and to the evolution of the regional dynamic, reinforced by ethno-historical and economic-political perceptions of its unity (Whiting, 1993, 19). Even if it is currently forgotten or rejected, the geopolitical definition is still a crucial reference to the Caribbean genesis as a specific region. Apart from the divisions and fragmentation imposed by colonial legacies, cultural and linguistic differences, and the weight of the geopolitical confrontation, in the last few years a view of the Greater Caribbean has begun to emerge which is based on communalities – geographically centred on the Caribbean Sea; on convergences – predominantly political but also more and more cultural as shown by the holding of CARIFESTA (Caribbean Festival of Arts); and on confluences – largely related to cooperation and economic integration. In this framework the common problem and preoccupation, apart from differences and economic asymmetries, involves possible marginalisation from the international economic system due to the effects of the globalisation process.

The second dimension relates to the historical development of the socio-cultural, political and, or economic links that distinguish the region from the rest of the world. In this context in the initial phase and despite the limitations of some historical contacts across the cultural, linguistic and political divide, the Greater Caribbean has promoted several forms of cooperation between states through formal multilateral mechanisms such as the OAS (Organisation of American States) and SELA, along with recent free trade and economic cooperation agreements which we have analysed here and in other works (Serbin and Bryan, 1991; Bryan and Serbin, 1996).

Lastly the third dimension relates to the extent to which organisations have developed to deal with collective issues. A wide range of precedents exist for the creation of subregional schemes – CARICOM, the creation of CARIFORUM (Caribbean Forum), the Central American Economic System (CAES) and the Group of Three. The formation of the Association of Caribbean States is a comprehensive response to this dimension, based as it is on a wider concept of the Greater Caribbean and on an all-embracing vision of the region, although it is not yet 'a consolidated political actor' (Whiting, 1993, 19).

However regionalism means going further in the process of building a regional community. It means promoting an integration process that is more than the action of the states through intergovernmental initiatives. Integration has to be an endeavour to build a regional *social community*, not only through the consolidation of an interstate regional collective actor, but also through the development of mechanisms for participation in decision making by political and civil society, and the creation of a common collective imaginary incorporating a regional identity that is inclusive rather than exclusive[7]. This is the long term objective of regional integration – the forging of a community of shared values, common objectives and regional identity.

In the long term this objective can only be achieved through the process of building a distinctive regional identity[8] and the mechanisms that foster it. Although the geopolitical definition that created the Caribbean Basin became exhausted with the end of the Cold War, it was not necessarily the death knell of that definition or of the region it embraces (Maingot, 1994b, 5–19). In this formation process, the only common cause is the need for collective action to deal with the global transformations that are affecting the region. Individual options are ever more limited in a world of global economic, political, cultural and social change. In fact the *other*, which is now making possible a new definition of the region in terms of the Greater Caribbean, is the globalisation process itself. The definition of the region as part of a *contrasting narrative* threatened by marginalisation from the international system and even from the hemispheric system – due to possible exclusion from NAFTA and SAFTA – would seem to be making progress as a result of government initiatives and the expectations and initiatives of a broad spectrum of transnational social actors.

Notes

1   Based on the paper *Identidad cultural y desarollo en el Caribe anglófono: algunas reflexiones desde una visión antropológica*, presented in the seminar on *Identidad cultural y desarrollo en el Caribe*, Simón Bolívar University, Caracas, March 1987 and in the article *The Caribbean: Myths and Realities for the 1990s*, published in the *Journal of Interamerican Studies and World Affairs*, Summer 1990, Vol. 32, No. 2.
2   In a book on US policy on Latin America, Bob Pastor notes with a touch of sarcasm, 'This book is about US policy toward all of Latin America; but like US policy, it devotes a disproportionate amount of time to the Caribbean Basin. Some analysts argue that a wiser policy would concentrate more on Brazil than on Nicaragua, but I believe that such a wish will remain unfulfilled until Washington comes to terms with the "whirlpool" that draws it back to the nearer region' (Pastor, 1992, xi).
3   Erisman wrote in 1984, 'Despite the region's current high visibility and intrinsic importance, no book has been published for at least the last five years that probes in depth US policy toward the Caribbean Basin as a whole. This deficiency is perhaps partially due to the position taken by some specialists that the Basin conceptualisation is artificial because it assumes a degree of cultural and political comparability among the region's nations that simply does not exist ... Although there is some validity to this viewpoint, Washington has been treating the Basin as a policy entity for the past few years (with, of course, some subregional variations)...' (Erisman, 1984, xii).
4   As the same author adds in the mid-1980s, 'Puerto Ricans are too isolated and over-preoccupied with the United States to experience West Indianness. Fear and hostility exhaust the mutual awareness of Haiti and the Dominican Republic. Only the French, British Commonwealth and Dutch islanders – and the Cubans – have awareness of the West Indies, but the possibilities for cooperation are limited by linguistic and political barriers, and increasingly by ideological differences' (Clarke, 1985, 132).
5   For a more detailed view of the impact of the world situation on the region compare my work, *Should Latin America be interested in the Caribbean?* (Bryan, A. and Serbin, A., eds, 1996).
6   As a recent analysis pointed out, 'Although the intellectuals of the English-speaking Caribbean tend to reject the term "Caribbean Basin" because of its geopolitical implications, the term "The Wider Caribbean" is not very assimilable either as a means of referring to the 24 independent countries of the Caribbean Sea plus El Salvador. The term reveals a political philosophical concept in which

CARICOM is the inner core ... Circles are formed round the core. The first circle would be all the other islands that do not form part of CARICOM and in the second would be the countries of Central America, Venezuela, Colombia and Mexico. This concept implies an ordering and implicitly a valuation of the role of the countries in process of integration' (AEC, 1996, 1).

7 As Clive Thomas says on the failure of the Federation of the West Indies, 'First, a region cannot be integrated from above, by simply proceeding to bring together the existing governmental structures; second, the approach to integration cannot be one that sees integration as an administrative convenience; third, the capacity for effective regional integration of the Caribbean ultimately depends on the degree of development of internal political and social forces in the region' (Thomas, 1979).

8 Which some analysts identify, for example, with a *pan-national* and *transnational Caribbean identity*, as an alternative to the pan-national, pan-American identity promoted by the dominant elites in the US (Suarez, 1995, 142).

3 The globalising impact and regional reconfiguration[1]

'What happens to the hole when the cheese is gone?'
Bertold Brecht

The end of the Cold War has diluted the strategic importance of the Caribbean for extra-regional actors and reformulated the regional security agenda in line with new priorities of less relevance to global strategy (Serbin, 1993; Serbin and Tulchin, 1994). This change in the global balance has had repercussions on the negotiating capacity of the Caribbean's political elite and on elements crucial to the survival of national economies. The industrialised countries have now turned their attention to bolstering democratisation and market economies in the countries of Eastern Europe, to the building of the European Union or NAFTA; and to the dynamics of the relationship with Japan and the Asia-Pacific region. Moreover a series of international socio-economic and political processes is now shaping an increasingly interdependent and globalised international system and having a decisive effect on Caribbean societies in terms of economic, political, social and cultural transformations.

Economic globalisation

The economic transformation of the international system involves three basic processes – (1) financial globalisation with the transnationalisation of investment and capital flows; (2) the global restructuring of production, illustrated by the transition from the Fordist Taylor model to the more flexible, transnational Toyotist or post-Fordist model (Moneta and Quenan, 1994; Bernard, 1994), which links the economic globalisation process with the market economy, growing economic interdependence and liberalisation of international trade; and (3) the technological revolution, particularly information technology.

Globalisation has three other significant dimensions; (1) sociopolitical – the rescaling of the state imposed by the prioritisation of the market dynamic – the global drive toward the political homogenisation of Western democracy, closely associated with the market and the development of civil society with its own transnationalisation process; (2) communicational – the transnationalisation of communications through the technologies provided by the information revolution and the global spread of values and messages; and (3) cultural – the homogenising promotion of the values of Western consumerism at the expense of local expressions of identity and values (Moneta, 1994, 147–65).

The globalisation of financial markets, with an enormous increase in transnational capital flows, began to speed up in the 1970s following the collapse of the Bretton Woods system and the financial controls imposed to consolidate the welfare states. As Helleiner points out, this process reached maturity a few years ago when it began to play a significant role in modelling the structure and dynamic of the emerging political and economic global order (Helleiner, 1994, 167–73)[2]. The financial structure, as Strange notes, is an undeniable source of power, particularly in a market economy, since power is in the hands of whoever defines what credit can be created; in what form and amount; who has access to it; and on what terms. But control of finance also implies control of production (Strange, 1994a, 24)[3]. Economic globalisation 'results in a very rapid growth of international investment; its predominance over trade in services; the increasing importance of transnational corporations in international trade, along with the volume of intra-firm trade; and the appearance of extremely concentrated international supply structures, which crystallise into global oligopolies as a result of mergers and take-overs' (Moneta and Quenan, 1994, 15).

Financial globalisation has been favoured by several factors – technological transformation based on the development of telecommunications and reductions in the costs of international funds transfers; market pressures associated with the restoration of confidence in the security of international financial transactions; rapid expansion of demand for international financial services linked to the growth of trade and the activities of multinational corporations; availability of significant bank deposits following the rise in international oil prices in 1973; the trend to fluctuating exchange rates in the 1970s which contributed to the diversification of international investments in the face of volatile exchange markets; and the emergence of growing competitive domestic pressures that pushed financial operators into the international arena (ibid., 165–6).

The development of the post-Fordist model, though still limited in influence, is an important trend in the global restructuring of production. The model features new, more flexible methods of organising industrial activity (Bernard, 1994, 216–7) based on the global optimisation of the factors of production – equipment, labour, raw materials, stocks; integration of research, development, organisation of production and marketing networks; production of what sells based on continuous and detailed market research; and production of differentiated high quality goods with decreasing costs (Moneta and Quenan, 1994, 11). But the development of a flexible model of production involves transnationalisation. It means breaking out of the confines of a specific domestic market by interconnecting productive networks and adapting them to local markets. It affects the automation of production and the cross border spread of technologies, as well as the labour relations established by the Fordist model in the welfare state[4]. The post-Fordist model also has an impact on the negotiating capacity of the traditional labour unions and favours the establishment of intra-firm labour relations adapted to new technological conditions and the requirements of the restructuring[5] of production.

Together with financial globalisation the technological revolution, associated with information technology and the transnationalisation of communications, has limited the capacity of governments to regulate the transformations or, as some analysts caustically remark, even to understand them. Obviously the technological revolution is not limited to the field of information technology. It has generated a dramatic change in the previous technological paradigm (Watson, 1994a) and has implications in other fields such as bioengineering.

In conclusion, these three processes anchored in the transformations of the structures of finance, production and information[6] are the bedrock of the economic globalisation process. They affect the security structure established during the Cold War and stimulate an upsurge in world trade. In particular the growth of technological innovation in the transformation of the international system is generating a series of consequences related to information and its accumulation and control. These trends, in turn, are having concomitant effects on the redefinition of the traditional roles of the state and civil society.

The socialisation of globalisation – state and civil society

To adapt to new conditions under the pressure of the structural transformations taking place in the international economic system, states are being forced to implement structural adjustment programs to promote competitive integration into a new international division of labour. This process, however, is governed by the external pressures and demands for internationalisation coming from multinational corporations and international financial organisations, as well as by the ideological impact of neoliberal ideas, frequently linked to demands from the domestic technocratic sectors[7] for structural adjustments to consolidate the market economy as a basic international and domestic regulating mechanism. At the same time, the structural adjustment and restructuring of production generate tensions and conflicts within domestic sectors, particularly with respect to the dismantling of the welfare state and its associated social and distributive policies to make way for the regulating forces of the market economy, resulting in a transformation of political and civil society.

In this process, the sovereignty of the traditional nation state is affected externally – self determination and territoriality – and internally – popular sovereignty, legitimacy and consensus in the interests of the nation state (Camillieri and Falk, 1992, 254). However, as Cox notes, by acting as intermediary between the international and domestic spheres, the state not only does not lose its autonomy but in fact retains a significant part of it (Cox, 1987, 399–400). Even so it has to deal with a more complex and fragmentary set of actors and interests in the definition of its objectives. The state is split between, on the one hand, the dynamic of a world market – which transforms it into an actor in the market – and international policy – with the expectation of a continuing role as an homogeneous international actor in promoting its national interest; and, on the other, a special interrelation between the demands of domestic political society and its institutionalised actors – political parties, unions, legislatures – and those of civil society – social movements, NGOs, social networks – and their capacity to lobby and exert influence (Stubbs and Underhill, 1994d, 423).

The response to this multiplicity of demands, pressures and interests in terms of the state's own resources and potentialities is not a specific modality of state in the context of globalisation, but rather the development of many different forms of state (Cox, 1992, 143) based on the degree of internationalisation or localisation as a vehicle for the conflicts generated by the priorities and interests of all the different international and domestic actors (Camillieri and Falk, 1992, 254). In this context, states become *agencies of the globalising world* (Cox, 1992, 145) in their relationship with the market[8]. This has particular disadvantages for those arriving late in the process or in situations of structural vulnerability and asymmetric interaction or interdependence in relation to the states more directly involved in the globalisation dynamic.

No less significant is the consequent process of expansion of civil society and its transnationalisation, particularly in developing societies where the 'market economy plus Western democracy' equation is ideologically reinforced, along with changes in civil society's relationship with the established political society. In this situation, the civil society that emerges at global level is more than an actor, it is a 'context in which a great many groups form and interact'. The groups include formal representative organisations such as political parties, churches, trade unions and professional associations; formal functional organisations such as schools, universities and the mass media, and informal political and social networks ranging from local voluntary groups to social movements (Shaw, 1994, 648). As such, in a Gramscian sense, civil society is basically a battlefield where the hegemonic forces confront the counter-hegemonic forces.

Apart from the current debate on civil society, its differentiation from the state and its relations with the political actors – subjects we will not enlarge upon in this book[9] – what interests us here is the globalisation of civil society in relation to the emergence of *global issues* that unite the interests of different organisations and social movements through non-governmental transnational networks. In this way the process of global socialisation and interdependence generates a space for the emergence of new transnational agendas.

In general terms analysts agree on associating these movements, which form a global civil society, with issues such as civil rights, environment, gender and protection of the rights of indigenous peoples and so on. They form transnational networks with a growing influence on governments and state policies (Keck and Sikkink, 1994, 7–20), and are identified as critical alternatives to the globalisation process. These movements have undeniably been gaining ground in the promotion of issues on the global agenda and in their influence on the way issues are taken up by it. This has been done through pressure from non-governmental organisations in their relations with governments, intergovernmental bodies and international organisations, and even through pressure on multinational corporations[10]. Some authors even refer to a global dynamic between state and market, state and civil society, and civil society and market played out by transnational and domestic actors. But perhaps the most significant impact of the emerging conception of a global civil society, particularly in its liberal-pluralist version, is the promotion of democracy at international level (Macdonald, 1994, 275). This perspective, however, assumes a homogeneous view of global civil society and its development, which does not always coincide with the fragmented interests, priorities and perceptions of the social actors involved in the transnationalisation process.

This perspective also ignores the fact that global civil society reproduces the conflicts and contradictions of the domestic societies from which it emerges, and generates new conflicts and contradictions at international level (ibid., 285). Domestically this is particularly evident in the tensions that are generated in the institutionalised political society in democratic systems when the effectiveness and representativeness of political parties and unions are questioned, and culture and identity are emphasised. These attitudes frequently add to the fragmentation of society and to the difficulties in formulating broader projects and building a consensus around them. At international level, relations between non-governmental organisations and social movements in industrialised countries with similar partners in developing countries – on global issues – have resonance in domestic societies. These links create tensions, if not conflicts, between the financial and ideological power of the industrialised countries and the agendas of the developing world, without taking into account the structural inequality from which they emerge.

From this perspective, as Rosenau points out, we are clearly dealing with an international system that is increasingly marked by a *multicentric* and not necessarily *statecentric* dynamic as *realist* narratives have historically favoured; a system that is ever more complex because of the multiplicity of international actors and regimes that are attempting to regulate specific international spheres and spaces, and because of the transnationalisation of domestic actors, ranging from the state and the political system formed by the political parties and unions to the emerging civil society in all its varied social expressions[11] (Rosenau, 1990). At present both state- and multicentric models seem to be coexisting, leading to an array of scenarios for the development of the international economic system (SELA, 1993, 86–90). However, in addition to the proliferation of transnational actors, there are other perceptions and interpretations of globalisation in terms of the pace imposed on the actors in the process of intensifying international relations and interaction (SELA, 1994a, 5), with marked differences between the industrialised nuclei of economic dynamism and the peripheral areas.

Globalisation and regionalisation – the hemispheric effects

The economic globalisation processes linked to growing trade and interdependence are having a decisive influence on the emergence of economic-political blocs in the industrialised world, particularly in the form of three poles of economic dynamism (restructuring of production and technology, trade, and investment flows) – the

European Union (EU), the North American Free Trade Area (NAFTA) and Southeast Asia, focused on Japan. These processes create tensions between the dominant trend, towards trade liberalisation as the engine of development, regulated by the GATT and now the World Trade Organisation (WTO), and the moves towards the formation of regional blocs with the possible emergence of new protectionist temptations in the industrialised North. Yet, as some analysts note, globalisation and regionalisation are not necessarily incompatible since in the best of scenarios the formation of economic blocs can lead to globalisation based on regions – as long as protectionist measures are not intensified – through intervention by private actors in the markets, especially in the sphere of finance and international investment (Moneta and Quenan, 1994, 16).

The globalisation of finance and the consequent flows of capital and investment are having a significant effect on the restructuring of global production, which depends to a high degree on the capacity to finance the changes in organisation and production and the technological development that supports it. Because of this the regions with the largest flows and concentration of investment tend to concentrate the greatest potential for productive restructuring and competitive capacity in terms of global trade. In the new conditions of the international economic system, the highly industrialised countries are those that are the most attractive for investments in production. Moreover, as Smith comments (1993, 5), the regionalisation process is not limited to the promotion of economic processes, it also has a political dimension expressed in the political will to move forward with regionalisation – as is well illustrated by the evolution of the EU – which revalidates the approach of international political economy.

In fact the political and economic spheres are linked because the dynamic of domestic and international markets cannot be disassociated from state action – in its narrowest sense – in the domestic and international sphere. In a sense the market is itself a political mechanism that activates political conflict at both levels, in terms of who receives what, when and how (Underhill, 1994, 18–9). From this perspective, the state manages the domestic and international pressures by adopting domestic policies and undertaking intergovernmental negotiations, which are closely linked (ibid., 20). Increasingly the state is becoming a key interlocutor not merely in negotiations with other states, but also with firms and corporations in what Strange terms 'state-firm diplomacy' (Strange, 1994b, 107–8). In this context, the fundamental problem of international political economy is centred on the interaction between the transnational market economy and the competing system of states, in which the state, neoliberal discourse notwithstanding, continues to play a crucial role despite the *downsizing* process imposed on it in the new international environment.

In different conditions from those of the industrialised countries, economic globalisation has speeded up regional and subregional integration processes in Latin America. Earlier integration schemes such as the Andean Pact, CARICOM and the Central American Economic System (CAES), have been revitalised, and new schemes have emerged to form free trade areas in an effort to optimise economic spaces and maximise competitiveness. Examples are MERCOSUR, the Group of Three and the ACS[12]. By expanding regional economic spaces, these schemes increase intra-regional trade and develop economies of scale which contribute to a more competitive integration into the international economic system. In a parallel development, many bilateral economic complementarity agreements have been signed between the countries of the hemisphere[13]. Overall these processes have involved the development in Latin America and the Caribbean of what ECLAC has termed a process of 'new regionalism' or 'open regionalism' understood as a 'process of growing economic interdependence at regional level, spurred by preferential integration agreements as well as other policies in a context of opening and deregulation, as a means of increasing the competitiveness of the countries of the region' (ECLAC, 1994, 2)[14].

To a large extent these initiatives respond to a clear political will – in large part preceded and encouraged by the democratic political consensus created in the 1980s by the governments of Latin America and the Caribbean and which took shape in the Group of Rio (Frohmann, 1990), but which is also determined by the ideological ingredients of what is known as the 'Washington consensus'. These economic initiatives reflect the need – also political – for increased capacity for regional negotiation with extra-regional actors and multilateral organisations by harmonisation of policies; for the convergence of Latin American and Caribbean countries in the area of economic adjustment and restructuring processes; and for the redirection of their development strategies from import substitution to export promotion and adaptation to conditions of competitiveness in the international system.

Evidently the pressure for the transformation of the international system and concerns about marginalisation from the international economic system have stimulated the processes of economic adjustment, trade liberalisation and opening, and subregional integration[15]. These pressures have also led to a series of political reforms that affect the role of the state and political society, with significant social and political costs, generally under the banner of the neoliberal logic of the predominance of the market – whose outcome is apparently seen at the financial, productive, social, political and cultural level in the 1994

Mexican crisis. In this process the privatisation of state enterprises, deregulation, decentralisation and the reform of the state, dictated by the intellectual atmosphere imposed by neoclassical economic concepts, have gone hand in hand with the restructuring and cutting back of distributive mechanisms including employment and social policies which have affected different sectors of the population.

The *new regionalism* adopted by Latin America and the Caribbean means adapting to the *New rules of the game* (Moneta and Quenan, 1994, book title) in the international system, and deepening the earlier largely intergovernmental agreements into a more active participation and involvement of the business sector in the trade liberalisation and economic integration processes. This process requires a new linkage between the political elite, on one side, and business sectors identified with free trade and a new development strategy, on the other, in the context of the various subregional schemes. This new relationship does not always develop fluidly because not all the economic elite identify with the reforms, particularly in countries where the elite has developed in a protected market, with subsidies and assistance from the state as well as political patronage. Even so sectors of the political elite frequently persist in defending these mechanisms in the name of sovereignty and national interest, often in combination with a perception of the importance of territorial sovereignty which conflicts with the neoliberal views held by the technocratic elite educated in the industrialised countries and clearly identified with the transformation in progress.

In brief the socio-political effect of the transformation processes in Latin America and the Caribbean have forced adaptation to the new global economic conditions, and multiplied the actors affected. At the domestic level, in parallel with the multiplicity of transnational actors that have joined the states – intergovernmental and non-governmental organisations, multinational corporations, regional and global organisations, social networks – the economic and political reforms generated by the transformation processes have created new socio-political alliances and have marginalised traditional actors. These trends have affected national political systems and the possibilities of democratic consolidation in the conditions required for global restructuring. The capacity of the political parties and the traditional unions has deteriorated because of the difficulties in defining collective interests in increasingly complex and diversified socio-political environments – leaving aside accusations of adhering to political patronage and possible administrative corruption. Their capacity has also weakened because of the emergence of a range of social movements, based on specific social and cultural demands, which tends to dilute the boundaries of domestic civil society and contributes to the formation of a global civil society through transnational links with NGOs and other networks. In this respect much recent literature has described the emergence of new social movements in Latin America and their limitations in the political dynamic.

This set of transformations at international and hemispheric level is having a significant effect on the Caribbean Basin; generating a new kind of regionalisation process with a wider concept of the nations that should be included; and giving rise to a series of specific regional processes with the participation of new actors – not necessarily circumscribed to intergovernmental relations and interaction.

Regional security – the end of the geopolitical discourse as a regional catalyst

The end of the Cold War along with the globalisation processes in the economic and technological arenas have had a major impact on the Caribbean Basin. Since the late 1980s the region has seen the ending of the Central American crisis, the electoral defeat of the Sandinistas and, in the wake of the disappearance of the Soviet Union, the growing isolation of Cuba and the development of an economic crisis on the island. Despite the persistence of links with Russia and the inertia of the confrontation with the US – with the reinforcement of the economic blockade against the island with the passage of the Torricelli amendment in the US Congress and more recently the infamous Helms-Burton Law – Cuba has become increasingly isolated in the region and the glamour and attraction that characterised the Cuban model in previous decades has been replaced by a condescending solidarity among the neighbouring states and even some left wing sectors in the region. With this process the threat of a proliferation of socialist regimes in the region has disappeared for the time being.

The end of strategic bipolarity has weakened the region's strategic importance, made the emergence of alternative socio-political schemes more difficult, and reduced the capacity of the political elite to negotiate assistance programmes and preferential trade schemes – such as the Caribbean Basin Initiative (CBI), the Lomé agreements with the EU, and the CARIBCAN programme with Canada – in the context of their identification with the strategic interests of the Western bloc. The use of the so-called 'Cuban card' (Maingot, 1983b) to pressure the industrialised countries historically involved in the region, to maintain assistance and cooperation schemes, is consequently diminished. The new agenda of regional security, with nuances and variations, formulated, defined or implemented by extra-regional or regional governments, favours issues of secondary strategic importance – control of drug trafficking and migration; environmental issues; consolidation of democracy – in comparison with the weight that used to be assigned to the containment of the Cuban-Soviet sphere of influence.

This agenda is increasingly set by the domestic political dynamic, particularly in the US. A good illustration is the intervention in Haiti which was influenced by public concern in the US about illegal Haitian immigration, by elements of racism and by manipulation by the *black caucus* in Congress. The action was also aimed at promoting democracy in the hemisphere to the point of backing the restoration of a government that would – in other times – have been called 'radical' and probably 'pro-Communist' by US government agencies – although, in this case, democratically elected and with strong popular support. Similar observations can be made on the inertial effect of the confrontation with Cuba, influenced by the domestic political weight of Cuban-American organisations in the US and by public concern about the effects of an avalanche of Cuban immigrants. In short, under pressure from domestic elements in the industrialised countries, especially the US, the possibility that a Caribbean local political elite continues to obtain external assistance, through the schemes established during the Cold War, has disappeared or been severely reduced.

The definition of a regional security agenda is being hampered by growing domestic pressures from actors with dissimilar capacities, in conditions of clear asymmetries of power, and by varying perceptions of the emerging priorities. There is also – in the aftermath of the disappearance of the communist threat – the difficulty of establishing what threat or threats the regional states perceive which might justify a collective security system in the Caribbean Basin, based on convergent interests and concerns for the success of collective action. In this situation, it is no surprise that the ACS treaty does not contain any agreement for cooperation on matters of regional collective security in the traditional sense of the term (ACS, 1994b), or that the dominant discourse in regional security matters is shifting radically away from strategic military issues to police and intelligence matters. From this perspective, despite the persistence of border disputes and tensions between several countries in the region – including some maritime delimitations – the conceptual horizon of the region's security discourse does not include promotion of regional security agreements or mutual confidence-building measures (Serbin, 1993).

As Maingot accurately observes, the concerns of regional governments – and in a good part of the US – are increasingly focused on the problems of the internationalisation of corruption and violence; frequently aggravated by the collusion of bureaucratic and financial sectors with drug trafficking or organised crime networks, or terrorist groups. As a result, on one side, different modalities of international cooperation are being established in a bid to control these problems; while, on the other, criminal transnational networks are developing which could affect the political stability of the countries of the region (Maingot, 1994a).

In this context, financial globalisation and the information revolution are emerging as the first great challenge that the region has to contend with in the new global system – the incapacity of governments to control capital flows and the communications used for criminal purposes. The ease of transferring funds electronically facilitates the use of local financial systems, for money laundering and illegal movements of funds, by the drug cartels and other sectors of organised crime as well as by terrorist groups. This deepens corruption in local administrations since bribes are paid through mechanisms that governments and security agencies find difficult to trace and control.

Advances in communications technology are hampering state control of illicit activities and illegal networks. One Caribbean analyst calls this phenomenon 'computer terrorism' because it uses information technology to transfer information and capital, and often has a significant effect on the stability – not to say the honesty – of governments and officials. In short, the transnationalisation of civil society – which we will return to later – has led not only to the emergence of non-governmental networks and organisations on a regional scale with specific socio-political objectives and demands, but also to the rise of transnational criminal networks and organisations, which governments find very difficult to control.

In the social sphere, the weakening of the populist state and social programmes in general, together with structural adjustments in regional economies, have increased poverty and unemployment, particularly among young men; produced rising rates of violence and criminality; fomented regional and extra-regional migratory flows; and provided a ready supply of manpower not only for the domestic economy but also for transnational criminal activities.

The effect of this situation is not restricted to the expansion of local and transnational violence and criminality. It also creates a breeding ground for phenomena that have so far emerged only incipiently in the region, namely *ethnic and religious particularisms*. In an area of great racial and religious heterogeneity, where there are many significant precedents for ethnic friction – not to mention isolated incidents such as the attempted takeover by a group of Black Muslims in

Trinidad in 1990 – we cannot rule out the emergence of radical ethnic or religious movements on a regional scale[16]. These groups confer a sense of identity on the lives of broad sectors of young unemployed men trapped in poverty, by giving them a hope of breaking the vicious circle of anomie and frustration which the social impact of the adjustment programmes and state responses to globalisation often generate. In this context traditional notions, of sovereignty and national security and the historical discourse of regional geopolitics, are being questioned by the emergence of new situations that escape the state's capacity for regulation and control. These social phenomena have a marked transnational character as well as being *intermestic* since they link the domestic dynamics of violence with the transnational response of criminality. They generally outstrip the capacity for control and repression of the traditional police, military and judiciary, which are rapidly overwhelmed by the transnational nature of the phenomena particularly in smaller societies.

Simultaneously with the progressive decline in the strategic importance of the Caribbean Basin, the geopolitical discourse of national security, dominant in recent decades, is also being challenged – with its definitions and conceptualisations of the region – by the emergence of new security problems with novel characteristics. This discourse, which was traditionally associated with the region within the context of globalising demands and pressures from the international economic system, is being replaced among the political and economic elite by a more pragmatic discourse geared predominantly to economic issues. With this transition, the *geopolitical narrative* that defined the region has gradually become a *geoeconomic narrative*, although there remains a security dimension that is clearly identified with the effects of the economic processes under way.

From geopolitical discourse to economic unease

The structural transformation of the international economic system in the context of the globalisation process, which we presented schematically at the beginning of the book, is having a particular effect on the economies and societies of the Caribbean Basin. While this effect can be very different due to the marked heterogeneity in size, development and economic potential of Caribbean societies – particularly if we accept the regional definition of the ACS which includes Colombia, Mexico and Venezuela – it is still possible to identify some general trends in terms of the impact of the transformation and the strategies implemented in the region[17].

Table 1 Potential of the Association of Caribbean States, 1991

	Population 1000s	Total GDP (M US$)	GDP (US$)	Exports (M US$)	Imports (M US$)
CARICOM (1)					
1. Antigua & Barbuda	64.0	421.9	4 985.0	18.3	254.6
2. Bahamas	259.0	2 810.0	11 055.0	248.2	890.0
3. Barbados	258.1	1 696.0	6 572.0	150.6	699.0
4. Belize	189.4	395.6	2 089.0	134.0	235.0
5. Dominica	71.2	177.3	2 491.0	54.0	114.1
6. Grenada	90.6	210.1	2 319.0	22.0	119.7
7. Guyana	754.7	342.3	454.0	238.6	252.2
8. Jamaica	2 425.5	3 496.8	1 442.0	114.5	1 799.5
9. St Kitts-Nevis	43.0	170.9	3 974.0	32.1	108.6
10. St Lucia	154.4	421.4	2 730.0	109.8	297.0
11. St Vincent & The Grenadines	107.6	283.0	2 630.0	78.5	138.6
12. Trinidad & Tobago	1 237.4	5 278.7	4 266.0	1 985.0	1 667.0
Subtotal	5 654.9	15 704.0		3 185.6	6 575.3
Non-CARICOM					
13. Cuba (2)	10 732.4	13 415.5	1 250.0	1 090.0	2 646.0
14. Dominican Republic	7 321.0	7 197.0	983.1	658.0	1 979.0
15. Haiti	6 647.0	2 100.0	319.0	103.0	374.0
16. Suriname (3)	422.0	1 300.0	3 529.0	397.4	395.0
Subtotal	25 122.4	24 012.5		2 248.4	5 394.0

Table 1 (continued)

	Population 1000s	Total GDP (M US$)	GDP (US$)	Exports (M US$)	Imports (M US$)
Dependent Territories					
Dutch					
17. Neth. Antilles	191.3	1 210.0	8 464.0	186.8	951.8
18. Aruba	68.9	950.0	13 950.0	141.5	513.8
Subtotal	260.2	2 160.0		328.3	1 465.6
French					
19. Fr. Guiana	114.7	260.0	2 267.2	69.0	1 964.0
20. Guadeloupe	387.0	2 653.1	6 855.7	162.0	1 605.0
21. Martinique	345.2	1 500.0	4 345.3	246.7	1 949.4
Subtotal	846.9	4 413.1		477.7	5 518.4
United States					
22. Puerto Rico	3 294.0	32 469.0	9 857.0	19 440.0	21 765.0
23. Virgin Islands	101.8	1 340.0	13.2		
Subtotal	3 395.8	33 809.0		19 440.0	21 765.0
United Kingdom					
24. Anguilla	9.0	57.6	6 778.0	41.1	50.4
25. Virgin Islands	9.0	165.1	9 946.0	3.4	130.9
26. Cayman Islands	9.0	733.6	27 900.0	3.0	265.4
27. Montserrat	11.0	70.5	6 133.0	1.5	27.0
28. Turks & Caicos Islands	12.0	70.4	5 700.0	4.7	38.2
Subtotal	50.0	1 097.2		53.7	511.9
Subtotal	4 552.9	42 289.3		20 299.7	29 260.9

Table 1 (continued)

	Population 1000s	Total GDP (M US$)	GDP (US$)	Exports (M US$)	Imports (M US$)
Central America					
29. Guatemala	9 744.7	9 390.0	983.0	1 230.0	1 673.0
30. Honduras	5 298.0	3 900.0	754.0	808.0	864.0
31. Nicaragua	3 999.0	1 571.6	393.0	268.0	688.0
32. El Salvador	5 376.0	5 680.0	1 056.5	588.0	1 294.0
33. Costa Rica	3 065.9	5 570.0	1 805.0	1 491.0	1 698.0
34. Panama	2 476.3	2 000.0	828.0	377.9	1 514.0
Subtotal	29 959.9	28 111.6		4 762.9	7 731.0
Group of three					
35. Venezuela	20 227.0	71 100.0	3 519.0	14 892.0	10 101.0
36. Colombia	33 613.0	47 999.0	1 428.0	7 572.0	4 545.0
37. Mexico	82 997.0	280 000.0	3 386.0	27 121.0	38 184.0
Subtotal	136 837.0	399 099.0		49 585.0	52 830.0
Total ACS	202 127.1	509 216.4		80 081.6	101 791.2

Source: Prepared by the Centro de Investigación Económica para el Caribe (CIECA) based on information from the Caribbean Development Bank (CDB), the Economic Commission for Latin America and the Caribbean (ECLAC), the Inter-American Development Bank (IDB) and C/LAA.

Notes:
(1) Montserrat is included with the dependent territories.
(2) Estimate made in CIECA as official figures for Cuba were not available.
(3) Suriname became a member of CARICOM in 1995.

As a general reaction to the debt crisis of the 1980s and to international pressures, the majority of the countries of the region opted to redefine or adopt new development strategies to replace the policy of *import substitution*, which had been combined with active state intervention to protect domestic markets. The new strategies were based on promotion and diversification of exports, with a complementary effort to improve competitiveness in the international economic system by adopting economic adjustment and restructuring programmes[18]. The programmes sought to slim down the excessive role of the state in the economy and stimulate private investment in production by emphasising the logic and expansion of the market[19].

Aside from their size and economic potential, Caribbean economies have been characterised by exploitation of natural resources and production of agricultural and semi-manufactured products with little value added, limited diversification and an epidemic of what is known as the 'Dutch disease'[20]. This is the context in which the new challenges created by financial globalisation, the technological revolution and the global restructuring of production have generated a series of transformations associated with the structural adjustment process. The response to the economic globalisation process has been to reduce and redefine the conventional functions of an excessively large state, traditionally shored up by political patronage, influence peddling and populist pacts (Payne, 1993). This has been done by public spending cuts, privatisation, deregulation and sometimes – not always fully developed – economic opening and liberalisation combined with fiscal and monetary macroeconomics policies consonant with the need to project an image of reform and economic stability and to create an attractive climate for foreign capital and technology based on export diversification and competitive capacity. The process had four specific consequences.

Firstly to attract foreign investments the state had to develop the necessary fiscal conditions, infrastructure, and training and labour schemes. (The effect was especially evident in the export processing zones set up in the Dominican Republic, Jamaica and Puerto Rico[21].) Secondly the state had to become an effective – and valid – interlocutor for the transnational corporations that might be interested in investing in the country. Thirdly the state had to create the right conditions, to stimulate and develop the local private sector, by recycling it from small local production to competitive exports. Lastly in the sociopolitical sphere, the search for transnational partners and capital forced the state to water down existing social and political contracts, in terms of their capacity to distribute resources through social policies and to regulate labour relations, with significant social and political costs.

In spite of the positive effects of the export processing zones on economic growth, the investments attracted by the low labour costs and tax breaks have led to the establishment of assembly industries with minimal requirements for skilled labour – which leads to the recruitment of a female labour force and creates a gender imbalance. This is a paradoxical outcome during a period when the restructuring of global production is strengthening the demand for advanced technology and skilled manpower, and the dynamic of world trade is increasingly centred on trade in manufactures with high value added, and services. In addition, because of the regionalisation processes in the industrialised countries and possible protectionist threats, this reorientation is leading to an expansion of regional economic spaces in an effort to increase intra-regional trade, develop economies of scale, and expand markets and foreign trade as a means of avoiding marginalisation from the international economic system.

In the case of the small countries of the Caribbean Basin in general, and the insular non-Hispanic Caribbean in particular, this process is especially urgent because of the possible disappearance of preferential trade agreements, such as the Caribbean Basin Initiative with the US, the Lomé agreements with the EU, and CARIBCAN with Canada. Another potential threat to the entry of Caribbean products into the US market comes from Mexico's competitive advantage following its membership of NAFTA (Gill, 1993 and Lewis, 1994). The perception of the smallness of their domestic and subregional markets makes them less attractive for foreign investments and reinforces the process. As a result specific recommendations have been made for expanding the economic space through free trade and economic complementarity agreements (West Indian Commission, 1992). At the same time, bearing in mind the differences of scale, similar concerns prompted Mexico, Colombia and Venezuela to create the Group of Three – despite each country's different priorities, objectives and expectations from the initiative, which we have analysed elsewhere (Serbin and Romero, 1993).

The promotion of free trade agreements is producing a need for policies to stimulate the active participation of the business sectors in the *new regionalism*, discussed earlier. The development of intergovernmental agreements involves a significant transfer of sovereignty because of the need for the harmonisation of macroeconomics policies if processes are to move forward. Foreign policies – especially in the area of trade – also have to be coordinated to foment solid relations with extra-regional actors or schemes such as NAFTA and the EU. The new role required of the governments of regional states links domestic and international processes to generate a series of socio-political consequences involving a multiplicity of actors.

The socio-political impact of globalisation and regionalisation

The reshaping – when not in fact downsizing – and the internationalisation of the state in the Caribbean Basin is having specific political and social repercussions.

Firstly the reduction of the state and its traditional role in the economy is generally associated with the end of the social-political contract, which depended on the state's use of the resources obtained from foreign assistance, and the export of products on preferential terms, to adopt policies in favour of certain social sectors (Dominguez, 1993). This system is widespread in the non-Hispanic insular Caribbean and Cuba, but not in Central American countries, as was illustrated by the polarisation and the social conflicts that broke out in that area in the 1970s (Huber, 1993). It is also reflected to some extent, given their economic particularities, in the populist policies of the PRI in Mexico and in the Venezuelan democratic system, but less so in the case of Colombia.

Considering that societies in the region have been generally sustained by patronage and populist political systems, the foreign debt crisis and the adjustment programmes that followed it have prompted a clear reorientation of state policies. This shift has been directed, as noted earlier, toward support for development of the private sector as the driving force of economic growth and the export strategy. However, a distinction must be made within the domestic private sector, which was generally formed in the heat of protectionist policies and state subsidies[22], between the sectors with capacity for competitive international adaptation, and other sectors strongly established in the domestic market and reticent about the opening.

Secondly along with the political dialogue needed to promote the active commitment of the domestic business sectors, the state, and through it the political elite in the government, has had to establish negotiations and create links with multinational corporations – to attract capital and technology; with international financial agencies – to renegotiate the foreign debt as part of the structural adjustment prescribed by them and to obtain additional credits; and with other governments and intergovernmental mechanisms – to promote free trade and economic cooperation agreements in a bid to increase trade and attract investments.

In this growing dialogue with domestic and international economic factors, the linkage between the traditional political elite and the emerging technocratic sectors has been decisive. The technocrats have contributed the know-how needed to make the economic adjustment and liberalise trade, and provided the necessary legitimisation with the international interlocutors. In short the linkage between the political and technocratic elite, and domestic and international corporate interests – possibly in conflict – has formed a hegemonic sector which has amply benefited from the process due to the interdependence of domestic and transnational interests.

In this framework, under pressure from external demands and the need to implement rapid and efficient economic reform policies to raise international competitiveness, particularly during the height of the implementation of neoliberal policies in the late 1980s, the demands and expectations of the population have been relegated to second place and the social and distributive policies associated with them have tended to decrease. This trend has generated political and social tensions which have prevented the building of a consensus around the reform projects and the new development strategies. At the same time the speed and efficiency required by the international actors in the implementation of these programmes has thwarted the formulation of medium- and long-term policies that could have progressively compensated for the difficulties, and has held up the implementation of industrial and research policies to improve long-term international competitiveness, based on a restructuring of production.

Consequently, from the socio-economic and socio-political points of view, the adjustment programmes entail, in their first stage, a significant expansion of the range of losing groups and sectors in Caribbean societies. The sectors affected by the new economic policies include a large part of the rural population – eliminating subsidies and lowering international prices for agricultural products (cf. Kaiser, 1994); public administration and state enterprises – cutting state spending and weakening the unions in the public administration; the unionised movement in general – relaxing labour regulations to attract foreign investments, for example in the export processing zones; unskilled female workers – combining low-cost labour with impaired workers' rights in the new nuclei of production; and the low-income sectors in general – worsening their poverty with the elimination of social policies, and the growth of unemployment and underemployment in an expanding informal economy.

The most evident socio-political costs of this general process are reflected in several ways. Firstly there is weakening support for traditional political parties – no longer able to deliver the benefits of the system of spoils and political patronage and increasingly identified with corruption scandals which would probably have been overlooked or played down in boom times, and the already noted disintegration of the unions – which had founded their own political parties in some countries of the region. Secondly there is a proliferation of social movements with specific demands to compensate for the incapacity of political organisations to articulate sectional interests (Deere, 1990). In this respect there has been a significant development of community based organisations, neighbourhood associations, women's groups, religious organisations, environmental movements and human rights groups all over the Caribbean. These movements have had a considerable impact on the proliferation of civil society and its influence on governmental bodies and agencies, as well as on the channels of institutionalised political expression such as political parties, unions and legislatures. However the expansion of these social groups has fragmented their popular support and, on the political-institutional level, weakened their capacity to unite people, articulate interests and develop a consensus with the traditional political parties and unions.

In brief, a radical redefinition has taken place of the social and political contracts that had formed the scaffolding for the consolidation of the region's democratic systems, bolstered by different distributive modalities. This change has had a clear impact on the legitimacy and viability of the systems of government and of governance itself.

From the socio-political and economic point of view, the adjustment programmes, particularly in their early stages, have involved a vicious circle that few of the political elite have forseen or known how to break out of in time. This is well illustrated by the successive crises in Venezuela and the financial crisis in Mexico – preceded by the Chiapas rebellion and the assassination of presidential candidate Colosío – but the process can also be seen in the rest of the Caribbean Basin. The credibility and legitimacy of the institutionalised mechanisms of expression in the political system are being seriously affected by the political tensions emerging between the *modernising* bloc formed by the political and economic elite, the technocratic bureaucracy and external interests, on one side, and the sectors affected directly or indirectly by the social and political costs of the reduction and redefinition of the state, on the other.

These democratic deficiencies are having a serious effect on the state's capacity to govern in a deeper sense than the mere existence of more or less consolidated democratic political cultures in the majority of these countries. (These democracies range from the Westminster parliamentary model adopted in the English-speaking Caribbean to the presidential variations in Latin America, based on one-, two- or multi-party systems.) The internationalisation of the state and of political and civil society in the globalisation process are transferring this democratic deficit to the regionalisation process now under way.

Notes

1. Based on the central paper of the seminar *La agenda sociopolítica de la integración en el Caribe*, organised by FLACSO-República Dominicana, Santo Domingo, March 1995, and on the article *Los desafíos del process de regionalización de la Cuenca del Caribe: integración, soberanía, democracia e identidad*, Revista Venezolana de Economía y Ciencias Sociales, No. 4, October–December 1995.
2. In his analysis the author adds that this process not only involved a dilution of Keynes' and White's ideas on protection by a welfare state associated with the establishment of Bretton Woods, but favoured the preservation of the autonomy of US policies in dealing with its growing external and internal deficits, reinforcing its hegemonic position in the new global financial system.
3. For a more extensive analysis see Strange (1988).
4. Moneta and Quenan conceive the Fordist model 'as a coherent whole that crystallised in certain forms of management and business organisation on the basis of four fundamental principles. First, reduce and rationalise operating times thanks to strong mechanisation and the synchronisation of productive flows. Second, establish a strict hierarchy between concepts, organisation and sales, in which the first commands the global process. This was the result of the third principle, that goods produced in mass and at low cost always found a sustained demand, even when their quality was mediocre (which relativised the role of the marketing and advertising). Lastly, the large corporations reserved for themselves the stable part of demand, while smaller producers had to contend with the fluctuations of the markets or satisfied the demand for differentiated products and in small series' (Moneta and Quenan, 1994, 10–11). The model was based on a domestic demand that was stabilised in internal markets through agreements on the welfare state and on labour relations which linked wages to productivity (Bernard, 1994, 218; Lipietz, 1994, 29). But perhaps the most significant element of the model for our purposes is the close relationship between Fordism and national space, since its evolution in the US after the second world war was marked by a relationship with a defined national market (ibid., 218 and 29).
5. In fact it involves the destruction of the unions as political forces and their substitution by 'pro-management company-based labour unions that acted as an unofficial administrative arm of management' (Bernard, 1994, 219).
6. Here we follow Strange's classification (1988 and 1994a).
7. Compare Bierstecker (1992, 115) who suggests that in an integrated perspective it is the need to integrate the four aspects in the analysis of the factors, that determines structural changes.
8. Samir Amin goes further in a view that suggests that these processes bring with them two new elements, 'the deterioration of the centralised nation-state and the subsequent disappearance of the link between the sphere of reproduction and accumulation and that of political and social control, which until now had been precisely determined by the borders of this centralised nation-state; and the decline of the contrast between central industrial regions and non-industrialised peripheral regions, and the emergence of new dimensions of polarisation' (Amin, 1994, 120).

9   Compare Cohen and Arato (1992) and for a more recent criticism from Marxist or post-Marxist positions, Vilas (1994) and Macdonald (1994). As a working definition of civil society, we use the one provided by Diamond, 'the realm of organised social life that is voluntary, self-generating, (largely) self-supporting, autonomous from the state, and bound by a legal order or set of shared values (which) involves citizens acting collectively in a public sphere' (Diamond, 1994, 5).

10 Keck and Sikkink refer, for example, to the world campaign against Nestlé and the baby food produced by that multinational (Keck and Sikkink, 1994, 7–20).

11 Parry (1994) refers to the clash between a view of 'one-world politics' versus a view of 'the world in pieces', which in essence is a reference to the ongoing debates between neorealists and neoliberals. (Cf. among others, Keohane, 1986; Baldwin, 1993; Powell, 1994).

12 See the CEPAL and SELA documents on integration processes (CEPAL, 1994b; CEPAL, 1994a; SELA, 1994d).

13 As a recent CEPAL document stated, 'The new generation of agreements presents marked differences with those made in the last decade. They generally promote the establishment of free trade for virtually all trade in very short periods, and they usually add interesting linking elements in the area of infrastructure interconnection, facilitation and promotion of mutual investments and trade in services, as well as flexible mechanisms for dispute settlement, among others. These agreements usually unite countries with similar orientations in their trade and economic policies, or with other nearby countries, with which important economic links already exist' (CEPAL, 1994b, 5). At the date of the document CEPAL had identified twenty six economic complementarity agreements of this kind.

14 The open regionalism displayed in the region is also seen as an alternative to the possibility of increased protectionist measures by the industrialised countries, constituting an 'important function, in this case a defence mechanism against the effects of possible protectionist pressures in extraregional markets' (ECLAC, 1994).

15 The 'Washington consensus' is mainly reflected in the general disposition of regional governments to promote structural adjustment programs (Cf. Hurrell, 1992).

16 There are numerous precedents in the context of the development of black nationalist movements associated with Black Power in the non-Hispanic Caribbean which we have analysed elsewhere (Serbin, 1987), as well as similar movements including indigenous ones in the Caribbean Basin as a whole.

17 Compare the CEPAL and SELA documents quoted and, for the specific case of the insular Caribbean, with special reference to the members of CARICOM, Quick (1993) and Watson (1994).

18 The obvious model for the development of these strategies was the Newly Industrialised Countries (NICs) of Southeast Asia, based on their successful implementation of outward-looking development strategies through export promotion. However, the role played by the state prior to their economic take-off through industrial and research policies, development of infrastructure and training of human resources is often overlooked. Compare, on the adjustment programmes in the CARICOM countries, Worrell and Bourne (1989); Caribbean Development Bank (1993); World Bank (1994); and, for Central America, Sojo (1995).

19 Basically the structural adjustment involves a reduction and redefinition of the economic intervention of the state in the economy, in association with a growing emphasis on the market for the allocation of goods and scarce resources (Bierstecker, 1992, 108).

20 Quick defines 'Dutch disease' as the situation in which 'a very small country finds a ready world market for one product, the export boom in that product pulls local resources away from other industries and undermines their competitiveness' (Quick, 1993, 216). Despite the reference to small countries, the same pattern can be observed in the case of Venezuela.

21 In the case of some Caribbean countries (Dominican Republic, Haiti, Jamaica), these policies led to the implementation of export processing zones (EPZ) to attract foreign investments through tax exemptions and more flexible labour regulations, taking advantage of the interest of multinational companies in geographical proximity to the US market, the opportunities opened by the Caribbean Basin Initiative and the US Generalised System of Preferences, the availability of an unskilled work force, low wages and the absence of tax or labour restrictions, with the backing of the respective government. However the establishment of EPZs also depends on the interest of the multinational companies in benefiting from proximity, using available supplies in favour of their own trade and financial dynamic, and negotiating with the respective governments. These policies do not necessarily result in transfers of technology, or development of production with significant value added, or the training of more skilled human resources (cf. Hillcoat and Quenan, 1991).

22 Watson specifically mentions that in the English-speaking Caribbean there is only a mercantilist business sector, incapable of adapting to the competitive conditions imposed by global productive restructuring and unable to transform themselves into effective engines of economic growth (Watson, 1994c, 15–6). Quick (1993) also refers to the limitations of the Caribbean business sector.

4 | The process of regionalisation in the Greater Caribbean[1]

'Water that is too pure has no fish'
Ts'ai Ken T'an

Intergovernmental regionalisation – the Association of Caribbean States

On July 24, 1994, in Cartagena de Indias, the Association of Caribbean States (ACS) was founded with the participation of twenty five independent states as full members and twelve associated states as associated members. The aim of the new regional grouping was to create a free trade area among the countries of the region, harmonise their policies toward third parties and promote functional cooperation (Constitutive Agreement of the ACS, 1994). Paradoxically although the principal promoters of the initiative are the member states of CARICOM, the ACS is a response to a *wider vision*[2] of the region as the *Caribbean Basin* or *Greater Caribbean*, with strong resonances of the *Third World* definition in fashion in the 1970s, since its member states are characterised as developing countries and, for the time being at least, the US and its associated states[3] are not included. The initiative, which is a clear response to recent global and hemispheric transformations, has the active support and participation of the members of the Group of Three (Mexico, Venezuela and Colombia) and the backing of the Central American countries. For the first time a regional scheme that includes all the countries of the region has been set in motion.

However in addition to the existing questions surrounding the process, some new ones are emerging on whether the vision behind the initiative is an effective response to the aspirations of Caribbean societies. The ACS expands subregional economic spaces, through free trade agreements, as a means of strengthening the region's future possibilities. The Central American Common Market (CACM) and the economic integration process in that area were reactivated in the early 1990s with the creation of the Secretariat for Central American

Integration (SICA), after the culmination of the regional pacification process that followed the signing of the Esquipulas Agreement and the efforts of the Contadora Group. CARICOM was similarly reactivated, particularly from 1989 onwards. The aim of these processes, along with the creation of the Group of Three in 1989, was to promote, expand and multiply subregional free trade agreements. The three schemes, together with the inter-scheme agreements and bilateral agreements between Cuba and the Dominican Republic, laid the groundwork for the formation of the ACS in July 1994.

The ACS is an 'organisation for consulting, coordination and co-operation' (ACS, 1994, 6). Its fundamental objectives are to promote a free trade scheme in the Caribbean Basin, harmonise policies in relation to third parties and foster functional cooperation within the framework of a general strategy for the promotion of regional integration. In this respect the ACS is a clear response to the dominant orientation of the region's political and governmental elite in the sense of increasing intra-regional trade, cooperation and coordination in all areas, in the context of the processes of globalisation and regionalisation taking place in the international system. A superficial analysis of the documentation that led to the creation of the ACS shows very clearly that one of the principal referents for the process was the formation of NAFTA and the launch of the Initiative for the Americas (IFA) by

Table 2 *Potential of the ACS (1991) by Groups of Member Countries*

Groups of countries	Population (1000s)	GNP (M US$)	Per capita GNP (US$)	Exports (M US$)	Imports (M US$)
CARICOM	5 655	15 704	2 777	3 185.6	6 575.3
Non-CARICOM	25 122	24 013	956	2 248.4	5 394.0
Dependent territories (1)	4 553	42 289	9 212	20 299.7	29 260.9
Central America	29 960	28 112	938	4 762.9	7 731.0
Group of 3	136 837	399 099	2 917	49 585.0	52 830.0
ACS total	202 127	509 217	2 516	80 081.6	101 791.2

Source: Prepared by CIECA with information from the Caribbean Development Bank (CDB), the Economic Commission for Latin America and the Caribbean (ECLAC), the Inter-American Development Bank (IDB) and C/LAA.

Notes:
(1) Includes the associated territories of the United Kingdom – Virgin Islands, Cayman Islands, Turks and Caicos Islands, Anguilla and Montserrat; associated states of the Netherlands – Federation of the Netherlands Antilles and Aruba; French Overseas Departments – Guadeloupe, Martinique and French Guiana; and US associated states – Virgin Islands and Puerto Rico.

President Bush in 1990[4]. These events strongly influenced the initiative promoted by CARICOM and supported by other countries in the region which led to the creation of the ACS – a new subregional scheme in the already complex mosaic of bi- and multilateral initiatives at hemispheric level.

As one analyst noted, the ACS is a proposal for the unification 'of efforts, resources and objectives already existing in five regional groupings at different levels of institutional and organisational development' (Lewis, 1995, 14). These are (1) the group of CARICOM member states; (2) the group of states in the CACM and SICA; (3) the Group of Three – Mexico, Venezuela and Colombia; (4) the independent states not integrated into any scheme – Cuba, the Dominican Republic, Haiti and Suriname[5] – but which maintain various modes of cooperation with the other countries of the region; and (5) the dependent territories, associated states and overseas departments of Great Britain, Holland, the US and France (ibid.).

In terms of its diverse actors, interests and perceptions, this new initiative assumes, in general terms, a new conceptualisation of the Caribbean Basin subregion understood as the Greater Caribbean, which emphasises the community of interests of the insular and coastal Caribbean nations; the overcoming of the divisions inherited from the colonisation process; the need to maximise the economic and political advantages of the geographic community; and the urgency of promoting forms of cooperation that help to prevent marginalisation and facilitate integration into an international economic system whose dynamism springs fundamentally from the three large economic blocs of North America, the European Community and Southeast Asia. A new perception of the geopolitical and geoeconomic reconfiguration of the subregion, closely related to the Third World definition of the Caribbean Basin fashionable in the 1970s, is evolving on a geopolitical base where the regional actors are assuming a more active role (Serbin, 1994a).

In this context, the regional actors were in agreement on the need to create the ACS in its present embryonic state, in terms of three objectives, (1) trade liberalisation as a means of strengthening regional trade and the economies of scale necessary for integration into the international economic system; (2) strengthening the capacity for negotiation with third parties by forming regional strategic alliances based on the identification of common interests, in view of the dilution of the strategic importance of the region; (3) advance toward forms of cooperation and eventually of integration, by convergence around common interests and the consolidation of a regional identity to overcome existing divisions and heterogeneities, based on a common cultural and social fabric and in order to benefit the region's population as a whole.

However, different actors – governmental, intergovernmental and non-governmental – put different emphases on the priority and importance of each of these objectives. For some the creation of the ACS is urgent because of the need to deepen, in the short run, the trade liberalisation process already under way in the interests of promoting economic growth and the capacity for linkage with other economies[6]. In contrast others see the ACS in a broader perspective, as a means of increasing regional cooperation and integration in the economic and political, social and cultural areas taking into account the possible threat from exclusionary or protectionist forces at international level.

In terms of these perceptions – which form an increasingly complex and diversified spectrum of interests, spheres and levels of interaction and initiatives – the momentum recently acquired by the creation of the ACS poses a series of questions on its feasibility – in terms of the exogenous and endogenous conditions of the process and the difficulties and obstacles in its path – as well as on the assumptions underlying its creation and the roles of the different actors involved.

Background to the creation of the ACS

During the summit meeting of the heads of government of CARICOM member states and the presidents of the Group of Three, in Trinidad and Tobago in October 1993, a formal commitment was made to create an association of Caribbean states that would group together all the countries of the Caribbean Basin. The meeting agreed on a working timetable for the establishment of the association in July 1994.

This initiative had a series of antecedents. At the special 1992 meeting of heads of government of CARICOM, held to consider the report of the West Indian Commission, a first formal undertaking was made on the need to deepen and widen the regional integration process, and to create an association of Caribbean states, in response to the pressures from the ongoing economic globalisation process. The meeting was attended by observers from Colombia, Cuba, the Dominican Republic, Puerto Rico and Venezuela who welcomed the initiative[7]. Beginning in late 1992 and during 1993, CARICOM held a series of meetings to discuss successive reports on the creation of the ACS. The meetings culminated with the summit of October 1993 and the holding of a first meeting of CARICOM experts on the project in Barbados in early December 1993.

Table 3 Basic economic and social indicators of ACS member states

	HDI (1) ranking (1994)	Per capita GNP (US$, 1992)	Life expectancy at birth (years, 1992)	Literacy of adult pop. (%, 1992)	HDI (1) (1992)
Barbados	20	6 530	75.3	99.0	0.894
Trinidad and Tobago	35	3 940	70.9	96.0	0.855
Bahamas	36	12 020	71.9	99.0	0.854
Costa Rica	39	1 960	76.0	93.2	0.818
Venezuela	46	2 910	70.1	89.0	0.820
Panama	47	2 420	72.5	89.6	0.816
Colombia	50	1 330	69.0	87.4	0.813
Mexico	52	3 470	69.9	88.6	0.804
Dominica	64	2 520	72.0	97.0	0.749
Jamaica	65	1 340	73.3	98.5	0.749
St Vincent and the Grenadines	69	1 990	71.0	98.0	0.732
St Kitts-Nevis	70	3 990	70.0	99.0	0.730
St Lucia	77	2 900	72.0	93.0	0.309
Grenada	78	2 310	70.0	98.0	0.303
Suriname	85	3 700	69.9	95.6	0.677
Belize	88	2 210	68.0	95.0	0.666
Cuba	89	2 000	75.6	94.5	0.666
Dominican Republic	96	1 050	67.0	84.3	0.638
Nicaragua	106	340	65.4	78.0	0.983
Guyana	107	330	64.6	96.0	0.580
Guatemala	108	980	64.0	56.4	0.564
El Salvador	112	1 170	65.2	74.6	0.543
Honduras	115	580	65.2	74.9	0.524
Haiti	137	380	56.0	55.0	0.354

Source: UNDP, *Human Development Report*, 1994. (Reproduced in SELA, *Notas Estratégicas*, No. 5, June 1994, 5.)

Notes:
(1) Human Development Index.

In view of these developments in CARICOM, it could be inferred that the initiative came exclusively from its own member states following the recommendations made by the West Indian Commission to 'widen and deepen' the process of subregional integration, based on '... a transformation from perceptions of a Commonwealth Caribbean to those of a Caribbean Commonwealth' (CARICOM, 1993, 2)[8].

In this perspective, the December 1993 meeting of CARICOM experts emphasised the ACS objectives of 'economic integration and functional cooperation' in terms of, (1) promoting the liberalisation of trade within the ACS; (2) coordination, as far as possible, of policies in the field of external economic relations on issues related to NAFTA and in general on economic relations with third countries and groups of countries based on strengthening negotiating capacity; and (3) promoting functional cooperation in areas such as energy, the seabed, the environment, higher education, culture, elimination of drug consumption, language teaching, agricultural and industrial development, and transport and communications.

Simultaneously with these steps within CARICOM, the Caribbean Basin as a whole has witnessed, beginning in the late 1980s, different modalities of concerted political action, and free trade and economic cooperation agreements, which also have gradually been laying the foundations for the regionalisation process and a series of social processes. Colombia, Mexico and Venezuela formed the Group of Three (G-3) which evolved out of their experience in the Contadora Group in 1989. This grouping has the explicit aim of advancing toward subregional cooperation with the Caribbean and Central America and of creating a free trade area between the three countries (Serbin and Romero, 1993; Serbin, 1993). After solving a number of technical obstacles and political difficulties associated with the troubled domestic dynamic in each of the three countries, the G-3 free trade agreement was finally signed and came into force in the first half of 1994.

The G-3 agreement should create a pole of economic attraction, comparable only to that of MERCOSUR in the south. The creation of the G-3 was preceded and accompanied by a bilateral integration process between Colombia and Venezuela which began in 1992, and which includes a free trade agreement between the two countries. Until 1994 this process had developed into one of the most advanced processes of bilateral economic integration in the hemisphere.

In Central America Mexico laid the basis, at a meeting in Tuxla Gutiérrez in 1991, for a non-reciprocal free trade agreement with the countries of the isthmus aimed at the formation of a free trade area. Venezuela and Colombia are also seeking to establish similar agreements with Central America, encouraged by the advances made in negotiations with the Central American countries at the first meeting of the G-3 in Caracas in February 1993. In parallel developments the G-3 countries were granted observer status by CARICOM. Venezuela made a formal application to join CARICOM in 1990 and established a five year non-reciprocal free trade agreement with the grouping in January 1993 (Serbin, 1993), followed by a similar move by Colombia.

In relations with Cuba, the G-3 unsuccessfully proposed the resumption of the dialogue between the US and Cuba, in an attempt to mediate between the two countries, despite the embargo and the passage of the Helms-Burton Law by Congress (Serbin, 1994a). For its part CARICOM set up a Joint Economic Commission with the Cuban government in July 1993, which has generated negative reactions in the US (Erisman, 1995).

At that time, CARICOM's relations with Cuba led to a temporary cooling of relations with the countries of Central America, aggravated by competition for quotas for banana exports to the European market. However relations between the two groups began to mend after the end of the Central American crisis and the reactivation of the economic integration process on the isthmus based on the creation of SICA and the Secretariat for Central American Economic Integration (SIECA). In February 1992 a first meeting of both groups of countries took place in San Pedro Sula with the aim of promoting economic cooperation and a permanent ministerial forum was formed. In May 1993 a second meeting was held in Kingston where CARICOM and SIECA signed an agreement. A third meeting was planned for May 1994 despite continuing differences on banana exports (Lewis, 1995). In this context Costa Rica applied to CARICOM for observer status in May 1993. However due to the banana row, the May 1994 meeting was postponed until November 1996 when the need, for the beneficiaries of the Caribbean Basin Initiative in Central America and the Caribbean, to establish common positions on NAFTA parity, forced them to hold the new meeting, ignoring momentarily the differences regarding banana issues.

In the Spanish-speaking Caribbean, the Dominican Republic, which has been waiting for a response to its application for full membership of CARICOM since 1991, was interested in deepening its trade relations with the English-speaking islands with a view to becoming a potential *bridge* with Central America. Santo Domingo has increasingly identified with Central America (Lewis, 1995) as a result of frequent disputes with CARICOM following its becoming a member, with Haiti, of the Lomé Convention (Payne and Sutton, 1993)[9]. Currently however the Dominican Republic and Haiti have jointly established CARIFORUM with CARICOM members as a common forum for Lomé beneficiaries in the Caribbean.

This list of antecedents is evidence of intensified political and economic links and interactions between the governments of the

Caribbean Basin countries, as part of a continuing regionalisation process, which began at the end of the 1980s. The process is based on promotion of trade liberalisation in the framework of new outward looking development strategies and export promotion. The stimulus for many of these free trade initiatives has come from the business sectors, through their growing regional links and desire to expand economic spaces for trade and investment. Simultaneously, the regionalisation process in the Caribbean Basin is increasingly anchored in a rapidly developing *social community*, through the links and networks between civil society and non-governmental organisations.

In this context, the initiative for the creation of an association of Caribbean states not only finds fertile ground among the region's governments, most of which are identified with democratic political systems and development strategies based on export promotion, but also among several actors from civil society, which are receptive to a pan-Caribbean view that sets aside traditional parochialism and insularity. Even so these social actors do not always share the idea of identifying democracy with the market economy in the terms suggested by the economic and political elite.

However an analysis of the obstacles and difficulties that might lie in the way of the ACS initiative, and the convergences on which it might be based, requires an integrated approach which should include not only the economic and trade dimension, with an emphasis on trade liberalisation and financial flows in the framework of the existing asymmetries of size and capacity but also, (1) the geopolitical aspects, in the widest sense, in terms of appropriate positioning and the formation of strategic alliances, as well as supranational links that limit traditional concepts of national sovereignty; (2) the political issues, regarding the compatibility of the different existing political systems – and legal frameworks and traditions – and the possibility of a convergence of political wills on integration; (3) the institutional characteristics, taking into account the appropriate organisational structures needed to be established at regional level – the social dimension, with regards to the impact of the initiative on civil society and the reactions of its protagonists; and (4) the cultural framework, considering the possibilities of tempering the region's linguistic, ethnic, cultural and religious heterogeneities.

However the process, which is principally promoted by CARICOM and the respective governments and social actors, with the support of the G-3, Cuba and the Dominican Republic with different emphases and priorities, basically responds to a set of endogenous factors – whose more evident manifestations we have briefly mentioned – linked to a series of exogenous factors associated with the global, hemispheric and subregional context. These are the factors that are influencing the rise of a regional vision and the possibility of overcoming the heterogeneities, the confrontation and the asymmetries that characterise the Caribbean Basin.

Obstacles and difficulties in the configuration of the ACS

We have analysed in more depth elsewhere (Serbin, 1994d) the different expectations of the component parts of the ACS with respect to its significance and its relation to NAFTA. In brief, for the Central American countries and the insular Caribbean, the creation of NAFTA is eventually leading to the elimination of the non-reciprocal preferential trade benefits offered under the CBI, and to competition from Mexico in terms of access for their products to the North American market – because of Mexico's lower labour costs and more accessible transport infrastructure. Yet the generalised perception among ACS members in the early 1990s was that Mexico was a potential bridge to NAFTA and, from this perspective, a means of reinforcing regional negotiating capacity through concerted action and coordination of policies. The inclusion of Cuba, however, as pointed out elsewhere (ibid.), does not help the ACS to become a particularly attractive interlocutor for the US, at least in present circumstances or even in the process of creation of a Free Trade Area of the Americas (FTAA).

The asymmetry of economic potentialities, the diversity of priorities and objectives and the differing capacities for individual or subregional negotiation which characterise the Caribbean Basin countries associated with the scheme, do not augur well for fluid relations between its members. Although, as we noted, there have been approaches and efforts to cement economic ties between the Central American countries and CARICOM members, the former have tended to develop their own independent strategy in their relations with NAFTA and Mexico. At the same time, the lack of communication and transport links together with the traditional linguistic and cultural barriers have not helped to surmount the differences between the two regions.

In turn, at the beginning, the political crisis that led to the impeachment of President Carlos Andrés Pérez in Venezuela and the transition to the administration of President Caldera has interfered with the continuity of policy toward the Caribbean, and harmed relations with Colombia – the country's principal trading partner after the US. Relations with Colombia have also been aggravated by the flare up of tensions along the border due to the activities of Colombian guerrillas, and by Venezuela's unilateral move to establish closer links with Brazil and MERCOSUR. Finally Mexico's role as intermediary in the ACS, originally put forward for reasons of regional geopolitical influence and to counterbalance the relationship with the US, was severely threatened by the effects of the crisis of December 1994, with evident repercussions on its capacity as interlocutor in the ACS to foster multilateral relations with NAFTA and the US, if indeed that was a real possibility.

This situation is aggravated by the uncertainties of US domestic policy, with the Clinton administration's lack of definition prior to the Miami Summit and the electoral process in the US; the absence of a defined timetable for the creation of the hemispheric free trade area by 2005 and its slow and difficult evolution, and the changes that the Republican majority in Congress could make to the US free trade initiative. The best illustration of these difficulties was President Clinton's decision to provide 20 billion US$ in assistance to Mexico by executive order, to get around the difficult – if not impossible – Congressional approval of the 40 billion US$ aid package originally requested during the December 1994 crisis.

In relation to Cuba, perhaps there was some hope for a resumption of the dialogue between the two countries under pressure from business sectors in the US, despite opposition from the Republicans in Congress and their attempts to stiffen the blockade by penalising the island's trading partners – promoted by Senator Jesse Helms, chairman of the Foreign Relations Committee. The agreement with Cuba on migration, reached by the Clinton administration, the continuity of the meetings between both governments on the agreement, and permission for travel and remittances to the island could herald a change in attitude with a significant effect on the regional dynamic (cf. Preeg and Levine, 1994). However the passage of the Helms-Burton Law during the recent election campaign has set this process back, simultaneously alienating the EU and Canada from the positions taken by the US.

Yet aside from these developments in the US, the hemispheric dynamic is, at the same time, moving south with the rise of a *South American Free Trade Area* (SAFTA) built on MERCOSUR and ALADI – without the insular Caribbean and Central American countries – promoted by the Cardoso administration in Brazil, in the context of a significant reactivation of that country's hemispheric policy based on MERCOSUR, combined with closer ties with Venezuela and the Andean Pact. However the growth of intra-regional trade since 1991, which had emerged as an alternative to the possible marginalisation of the region from other regional blocs, and the closer political relations developed through the Rio Group are tending to increase the marginalisation of the small countries of the insular Caribbean and Central America at hemispheric level[10].

These difficulties, inherent in the domestic changes in some members of the scheme as well as in the US – particularly intense in relation to the institutional stability of some states – together with the dynamic of regional relations, have been accompanied by tensions caused by disagreements on the location of the ACS General Secretariat, in terms of the interests of the political bureaucracies which are strongly conditioned by the domestic political situations of member countries[11].

In this regard, during the first year of the creation of the ACS Henry Gill listed six problematic nuclei with regards to the organisation which create new challenges for the region, (1) the definition of an exclusive space which is not superimposed upon the objectives of existing regional and subregional bodies and integration schemes, and which is differentiated from NAFTA by assigning priorities to the Caribbean Sea as its central reference; (2) the definition of specific objectives, particularly in the area of investment and trade, aimed at coordinating the efforts of the various schemes with the interests of the ACS; (3) the delimitation of regional actors in terms of their participation and interaction, taking into account the central role that CARICOM has assumed and the special relationship of some states and associated territories with extra-regional actors – especially the French overseas departments, but also the possible participation of the US Virgin Islands and Puerto Rico; (4) the definition of a satisfactory budget in the present difficult economic conditions, especially of the smaller countries; (5) the degree of real commitment to the ACS of the full and associate members that signed and later ratified the constitutive convention of July 24, 1994; (6) a definition of the role assigned to the private sector, situated as interlocutor of the ACS in an identical limbo with the other *social actors* without any institutionalised participation in the process.

Gill had no doubt that there were still many important problems to be resolved in the process of launching the ACS relating to the definition of its aims, sphere of action, membership and the commitment of the actors involved in a process that is in full development. The list could also mention vagueness, lack of definition of institutional mechanisms and consolidation to spur the regionalising process (Gill, 1995, 11–5). However since the Port-of-Spain summit meeting in August 1995 the institutionalisation process of the ACS has been consolidated with the establishment of the Secretariat in Port of Spain; the appointment of a regional staff; the approval, by the member countries, of a budget, and the creation of specific committees and the holding of conferences on important issues, particularly trade. This process was strengthened by different technical and ministerial meetings, which culminated in the December 1996 ACS ministerial meeting in Havana.

Despite this situation and the uncertainty it generates, the initiative of the creation of the ACS is evidence of a growing trend toward regionalisation. The trend is expressed by the political and economic elite through intergovernmental initiatives of trade liberalisation – influenced by the uncertain hemispheric dynamic and the liberalisation of global trade – and by the societies of the Caribbean Basin through the creation of networks and spaces promoted by organisations and movements from civil society.

The social network of the regionalisation process in the Greater Caribbean

The regionalisation process is more than an initiative developed by the political elite of the region as a response to the globalisation process; to the geopolitical vacuum generated in the region by the ending of the Cold War; and to a search for a more beneficial economic – and collective – positioning in relations with the large economic blocs in terms of trade openings, regional cooperation and the speeding up of the subregional integration process with a view to the creation of wider economic spaces. It is also associated with a growing social, cultural, economic and political *interaction* 'which recognises the crucial role of mutual discovery in transcending cultural, economic and political barriers' (Girvan, 1990, 5), and generates, for the first time in the history of the subregion, the seeds of a 'social community' that develops transnational links between the different sectors of civil society.

This increasing interaction also takes the form of social and political projects identified with or differentiated from government initiatives by the emergence of new regional views supported by a network of relations and interactions between different sectors of the societies. New social actors and projects spurred by their own emphases and objectives are emerging to promote the regionalisation process, alongside the appearance of alternative spheres and circuits of interaction and linkage (Tomassini, 1989). They are forming a new regional fabric of transnational relations which responds to different expectations and goals, either identified with or antagonistic to the characteristics of the existing process of predominantly state-centred regionalisation (Banks, 1988; Rosati et al., 1990).

In short, the regionalisation process set in motion in recent years is associated with the development of a network of transnational relations in the Caribbean Basin which is frequently articulated through non-governmental channels, challenging the traditional role of the states; their foreign policies in regional relations; and their associated projects. In this context alternative projects are evolving in the new regional situation as part of the regionalisation process, and new networks of transnational interaction are developing and consolidating, creating the basis for an increasingly complex regional network.

Although the analysis is outside the scope of the book, it should be noted that this expansion of transnational relations with the progressive incorporation of a broad range of non-governmental extra-regional actors into the international system is one result of the globalisation process. A number of international organisations have played an important role in this including the United Nations Program for the Environment (UNEP) with a specific programme for the Caribbean (Jacome and Sankatsing, 1992), the Commission for Development and Cooperation in the Caribbean (CDCC) of ECLAC and UNESCO. A variety of non-governmental organisations has also been involved – extra-regional, in the case of OXFAM, and regional such as the Caribbean Development Policy Center (CDPC), Women and Development (WAND) and human rights organisations (Lewis, 1991, 1994; McAfee, 1991).

As a result international relations in the Caribbean Basin have developed over the last few years largely as a response to the growing influence of transnational actors in international relations at global level (Banks, 1988; Del Arenal, 1990) rather than exclusively to the regionalising dynamic promoted by governments. Even so despite the intervention of these exogenous agents, transnational relations, which are gradually making the network of regional relations more complex and giving it a separate identity, cannot be disassociated from the regionalising dynamic. They are a fundamental societal component of the different facets of the regionalisation process in the Caribbean Basin, which go beyond the explicit efforts of governments and their foreign policies.

In essence a specifically regional network of relations is evolving which is contributing to the development of a view of the Greater Caribbean as a region that transcends existing barriers to assume its own distinctive features, despite the inclusion of global issues on the agenda of contemporary transnational relations in the region – such as the growth of women's action groups, environmentalist associations, and groups promoting free trade and human and social rights.

Table 4 Caribbean Basin trade indicators, 1992

	Total trade in goods and services (A) (US$)	Total services (B) (US$)	Ratio B/A	Services credit/debit (US$)	Trade balance (US$)
ACS (1)	198 886.16	49 631.07	0.25	3 475.65	−23 830.75
CARICOM	15 995.56	6 983.87	0.44	2 211.25	−1 576.05
Bahamas	3 397.30	1 935.60	0.57	882.50	−841.20
Barbados	1 432.70	810.00	0.56	440.00	−306.70
Belize	604.60	219.50	0.36	54.30	−103.90
Guyana	Until '85				
Jamaica	4 385.40	1 875.9	0.43	488.90	−403.90
Trinidad and Tobago	3 690.90	1 033.4	0.28	−69.00	666.20
OECS (2)	2 484.66	1 109.47	0.45	414.55	−586.55
Antigua and Barbuda	797.38	415.78	0.52	221.28	−206.26
Dominica	225.12	73.04	0.32	7.22	−42.94
Grenada	237.95	114.84	0.48	38.32	−83.25
Montserrat					
St. Kitts-Nevis	247.33	123.27	0.50	36.65	−60.34
St Lucia	693.22	295.03	0.42	103.63	−152.63
St Vincent and the Grenadines	283.66	87.51	0.31	7.45	−41.13
G-3	150 496.00	35 273.00	0.23	−695.00	17 755.00
Colombia	17 260.00	3 967.00	0.23	−75.00	1 233.00
Mexico	101 042.00	25 333.00	0.25	2 359.00	−20 677.00
Venezuela	32 194.00	5 973.00	0.18	−2 979.00	1 689.00

Table 4 (continued)

	Total trade in goods and services (A) (US$)	Total services (B) (US$)	Ratio B/A	Services credit/debit (US$)	Trade balance (US$)
CACM	13 674.50	3 385.20	−0.25	177.20	−2 074.10
Costa Rica	5 469.00	1 542.80	0.28	174.40	−497.60
El Salvador	Until '91				
Guatemala	4 750.80	1 139.30	0.24	88.70	−1 044.10
Honduras	2 271.50	466.30	0.20	−29.50	−140.00
Nicaragua	1 183.20	256.80	0.22	−56.40	−392.40
Other Caribbean countries	18 252.10	3 989.00	0.22	1 782.20	−2 425.60
Cuba					
Dominican Republic	4 887.30	2 143.70	0.44	1 030.30	−1 612.00
Haiti	Until '91				
Suriname	734.80	121.30	0.16	−76.10	68.40
Panama	12 630.00	1 724.00	0.14	828.00	−882.00

Source: *International Monetary Fund Financial Statistics Yearbook '94*. Published in SELA: *Relaciones comerciales en el siglo XXI: Los retos que enfrenta la ACS*, August 1995.

Notes:
(1) Excluding dependent territories
(2) OECS (Organisation of Eastern Caribbean States) is part of CARICOM and included in the CARICOM total.

Transnational relations in the Greater Caribbean – the background

In the contemporary history of the Caribbean the political parties have been the non-governmental actors that initially made the largest contribution to generating transnational interactions and a regional view, in terms of ideological concepts and political projects designed to develop wider strategies and contacts, although generally with limited achievements. Historically relations between political parties and groups has fostered contacts with emerging leaders who have later joined their respective political elite and have contributed to the development of a regional view among the members of their own social group.

In this respect, in the 1960s and 1970s, the convergence of the decolonisation process with the process of ideological radicalisation of broad sectors of Caribbean youth led to the development of links and contacts between militants of ethnic and nationalist movements linked to Black Power in the non-Hispanic area, along with the development of links between Marxist-oriented parties throughout the region (Maingot, 1983b; Serbin, 1987). The links between the region's communist parties, based on relations between Marxist leaders and intellectuals, date back to the period before the Second World War. These relations took on special importance following the Cuban revolution and its regional projection with the emergence of the Sandinista government in Nicaragua, the New Jewel Movement in Grenada and contacts with Marxist groups and the revolutionary left in Jamaica, Guyana, Suriname, the French territories, the Dominican Republic and Haiti (Maingot, 1983b; Serbin, 1987).

The US invasion of Grenada in 1983, the Sandinista's electoral defeat and the eclipse of Cuban influence in the Caribbean Basin in the wake of internal difficulties and the collapse of the Soviet bloc have diluted this ideological identification which had developed with the region's radical political parties and groups in the 1960s and 1970s.

Also in the 1970s the increased interest of the *International Socialist* (IS) in Latin America, especially in Central America and the Caribbean, resulted in closer interaction between social democratic and socialist parties in both Spanish-speaking and non-Spanish-speaking areas. The participation of the People's National Party (PNP) of Jamaica and of Michael Manley in the IS brought about closer links between the parties of this orientation in the Caribbean Basin and closer personal relations between their leaders (Gamus, 1990, 80–1). These parties joined with parties in South America and Central

America to form the IS Committee for Latin America and the Caribbean in May 1980 in Santo Domingo[12].

The IS promoted the democratisation of Latin America and the Caribbean in the 1970s and 1980s, and played a part in the pacification process in Central America. It also stimulated contacts and interaction between the parties of the Caribbean Basin, despite their heterogeneity and differing degrees of ideological radicalness. The *Third World* atmosphere, which reigned at the time in the region, facilitated these closer contacts. However the US invasion of Grenada was a landmark in the revival of IS interest in the region because of the position assumed by the Barbados Labour Party (BLP), an IS member. The BLP backed the US action in Grenada under pressure from the Reagan administration (Williams, 1984, 297)[13].

The development of contacts between the region's political parties has also occurred among the progressive and nationalist parties through the Permanent Commission of Latin American Political Parties (known in Spanish as COPPPAL). Founded in the 1970s out of an initiative of the Partido Revolucionario Institucional (PRI) of Mexico, COPPPAL groups together political parties of progressive, nationalist and populist orientation from Latin America and all the linguistic areas of the Caribbean. With the global and hemispheric transformations, issues of subregional integration now take first place on its agenda (COPPPAL, 1992a)[14].

Paradoxically only a few political parties from the Caribbean take part in the Latin American Parliament, despite the participation of a large number of Latin American political parties, and the express wish to exclude the US and to include 'the Caribbean islands' (PARLATINO, 1992, 31). The Caribbean is represented by parties from Aruba, the Netherlands Antilles, Cuba, Haiti and the Dominican Republic. The presence of the Netherlands Antilles and Aruba in the Parliament may be due to the influence of Christian democratic parties, which are very active in the Dutch-speaking Caribbean and several of which are members of the Christian Democrat Organisation of Latin America (ODCA). The participation of these parties in ODCA is due to the activation of Christian democrat influence in the region in the 1970s, especially through links with trade unions of this orientation and training programmes for political and union leaders (Parker, 1988)[15] in the Dutch- and the English-speaking Caribbean.

Between 1994 and 1995, both the IS and ODCA reactivated their presence and commitment to the region. The IS organised a regional meeting in Haiti in early 1995 to back the establishment of democracy on the island, but with a wider perspective in terms of support for the democratisation of the region. ODCA also held a seminar-workshop on

The Caribbean in the 21st Century in September 1994, with the participation of a cross section of political leaders from the Spanish Caribbean as well as the English- and Dutch-speaking areas (ODCA, 1994).

Transnational relations in the Greater Caribbean and the business sector

An ECLAC document on relations between the Caribbean and Latin America reveals the existence of links between the private sectors of both regions, and stresses the need to prepare 'a comprehensive inventory of private-sector entities and NGOs in both regions' (ECLAC, 1992, 20) because of their crucial importance in promoting collaboration between the two areas. The colonial links of the majority of the countries of the insular Caribbean have encouraged the development of relations between organisations in a particular linguistic area with business organisations in the metropolis. An illustration of this is the link between organisations such as the Caribbean Association of Industry and Commerce (CAIC) and the Private Sector Organisation of Jamaica (PSOJ) with the British Caribbean lobby linked to the West Indian Committee (WIC) and the Caribbean Trade Advisory Group (CARIBTAG) which has formed a lobby group in the EC – the Caribbean Council for Europe (CCE) (*CA*, 1992b, 1) based in London.

Significantly, a business organisation from the Spanish-speaking Caribbean, the National Businessmen's Council (CNHE) of the Dominican Republic, was quick to join in this initiative based on its previously established relations with the WIC in the framework of the Anglo-Dominican Chamber and the Dominican Republic's membership of the Lomé Convention (*CA*, 1992c, 1).

Caribbean private sector organisations have expressed their concerns about the apparent incapacity of regional governments to promote a competitive and efficient integration of the Caribbean in the new world order first at the Fifth Europe/Caribbean Conference held in Curacao in November 1992 (*CA*, 1992d, 2)[16], and again at the Sixth Conference held in Santo Domingo in November 1994, to review the fourth Lomé Convention, analyse the advantages of the trade systems of Europe and North America, and evaluate the post-Lomé IV agreements which will come into force after the expiry of the present arrangement in 2000 (Caribbean Council for Europe, 1993)[17].

The most influential business lobby in the region is the Caribbean/ Central American Action Group (CCAA), formed in 1980 as a non-profit non-governmental organisation. During the 1980s, the CCAA developed a series of initiatives for promoting business interests and contacts in the region. Its annual meetings in Miami, attended by businessmen and senior government officials from the region, the US, Canada and Europe, make an important contribution to the expansion of business contacts in the Caribbean Basin. In the 1980s, the CCAA backed the consolidation of organisations such as the Caribbean Association of Industry and Commerce (CAIC) in the English-speaking Caribbean, and the Federación de Entidades Privadas de Centro América y Panamá (FEDEPRICAP) (*CA*, 1992d, 20).

Significantly, in December 1990, at the meeting of its board of directors in Miami, the CCAA transformed itself into the Caribbean/ Latin American Action Group (C/LAA) with the objective of including Mexico, Colombia and Venezuela in its sphere of initiatives and interests (*CU*, 1991a, 13). The groups fifteenth annual conference was attended by 'heads of state, business leaders, European ministers, cabinet secretaries, businessmen in search of markets and representatives of the US Congress', as well as officials and representatives of the Mexican, Colombian and Venezuelan governments (*CU*, 1991b, 1). A report on the NGOs in the region noted that C/LAA 'has led the way in the regional discussion of a post-preferential-treatment regional economy' (CRIES, 1991), promoting the development of free trade agreements and economic restructuring programmes in the region as part of the effort to create a hemispheric free trade area (C/LAA, 1991a; C/LAA, 1991b)[18].

During the last five years, this regional private sector initiative has been accompanied by other initiatives with a more focused scope aimed at promoting trade liberalisation in the Caribbean Basin. These initiatives represent a significant activation of relations between national business sectors in the region, along with the development of a network of transnational relations to promote the economic restructuring programmes and trade liberalisation under way in many countries. They are also evidence of a development strategy in which the business sector is tending to assume a more prominent role.

Non-governmental organisations and alternative projects

Despite the fruitful record of relations in the region in the 1980s already described, the traditional political parties and their associated unions are now being challenged by social movements and emerging non-governmental organisations. This process is associated firstly with the withdrawal and weakening of popular support for the more radical parties; and secondly with the incapacity of the more moderate parties and unions to mount an effective opposition to the social and political effects of the adjustment programmes (Deere, 1990, 96–7)[19]. As a result many of the groups and associations that emerged with the development of the informal sector of the economy are now capitalising on popular discontent and formulating alternative political and social projects. These projects are structured around the organisations emerging in civil society such as grass roots groups, community and neighbourhood organisations, women's groups, local development organisations and non-governmental organisations (Lewis, 1991, 232).

Aside from their local impact and possible national projection, many of these organisations are establishing transnational links, making proposals to reinforce regional identity and offering popular alternatives all over the Caribbean through the exchange of experiences and information, frequently with the backing of extra-regional non-governmental organisations. The contacts and coordination between grass roots and local development organisations, and regional and extra-regional non-governmental organisations has led, in many cases, to persistent criticism of the adjustment programmes and the formulation of alternative development *paradigms* based on popular participation and the formulation of political positions on development (Lewis, 1994, 130–1).

One of the institutions that has contributed most to this process of overcoming the linguistic, cultural and political barriers in the region is the Caribbean Council of Churches (CCC). The CCC was founded in 1973 as the first regional ecumenical association to involve churches and religious groups in issues and problems such as regional economic development, peace and strengthening the political capacity of popular sectors (Deere, 1990, 105). Under the influence of the progressive sectors of the churches and, in the case of the Catholic Church, of liberation theology, leaders involved in the CCC and associated organisations were very active during the 1970s among popular sectors, promoting education and political mobilisation, stimulating the creation of grass roots groups and communities and promoting contacts between all the groups concerned with achieving these objectives in the region[20].

Similar initiatives, of a more secular character, have been developed by the Caribbean People's Development Agency (CARIPEDA) through a network of local and non-governmental organisations, in the Eastern Caribbean, Puerto Rico, Jamaica and Trinidad, which promote development works and links with international agencies based on formulating and implementing strategies for alternative economic and political development (Deere, 1990, 103).

Other important organisations, particularly in the English-speaking Caribbean, are the Caribbean (NGO) Policy Development Center (CPDC), a network of regional, subregional and national NGOs which groups twenty one networks of non-governmental organisations in the region and the Caribbean Network for Integrated Rural Development (CNIRD) which promotes cooperation between organisations working with rural communities. Because of the important work done by the CPDC in recent years, its recommendations were considered by the *CARICOM Regional Economic Conference* in 1991, and in 1995 a proposal was made to grant consultative status in CARICOM to non-governmental organisations, employers' associations and unions[21]. These non-governmental organisations include groups concerned with development, churches, charities, credit unions, sports associations, cooperatives, chambers of commerce and unions (McAfee, 1991, 215). In some cases they hold inter-organisational forums with the support of unions or political parties, including the *NGO Regional Forum on the GATT*, held in October 1994, sponsored by the National Trade Union Council of Trinidad and Tobago (*CD*, 1994 and 1995) and the *Assembly of Caribbean People* held in August 1994 in Port of Spain (Assembly of Caribbean People, 1994).

Many cultural groups of popular extraction have been increasing their links through artistic and cultural encounters promoted by regional governments but which often spring from the action of popular groups. CARIFESTA which began in the 1970s, cultural festivals in the English-speaking Caribbean, in Guadeloupe and Martinique, in Cuba, Venezuela and Mexico have all created spaces for interaction where the issues of regional identity, frequently charged with criticism of economic programmes, have acquired special resonance, particularly in relation to the African cultural base which underlies the region's identity[22].

Since the 1980s one of the most active NGO networks in the Caribbean Basin has probably been the women's organisations. Starting with the UN-sponsored *Decade of the Woman 1975–1985* they have acquired a particular influence in the region in terms of the feminist agenda. Although many of these organisations have a local and national character, some of them, such as Women and Development (WAND) started in Barbados in 1978, and the Caribbean Association for Feminist Research and Action (CAFRA) started in the mid-1980s, have promoted research and action on women's problems at regional level, and have contributed to the growth of regional contacts and links between local organisations, as well as to the development of a regional concept of the women's movement. These initiatives have increased gender awareness at the level of the Caribbean Basin and fostered a Caribbean identity in the women's movement (Doñé Molina, 1991, 16–7). For example CAFRA covers the English-speaking Caribbean, Cuba, the French territories, Curacao, and Puerto Rico and the Dominican Republic, having evolved out of an initiative by Third World women grouped in Development Alternatives for Women Networks (DAWN) founded in Nairobi in 1985 (Deere, 1990, 112–3).

This feminist movement has recently become involved with environmental protection, another of the issues that has prompted the proliferation of regional NGOs. Environmental issues have been the rationale of numerous Caribbean Basin NGOs since the 1980s and have provided a framework for the development of a regional awareness of conservation. Some of the specific organisations involved in this area are the Caribbean Conservationist Association (CCA) in the English-speaking Caribbean, the Caribbean Environmental Health Institute (CEHI) linked to CARICOM, and a variety of academic initiatives including the Consortium of Caribbean Universities for the Administration of Natural Resources promoted by the Association of Research Institutes and Universities of the Caribbean (UNICA), research units on the environment and development established in the Universities of the West Indies (Barbados), Virgin Islands and the Simón Bolívar University of Venezuela, and the regional projects implemented by INVESP of Venezuela (Jácome and Sankatsing, 1992, 76–81).

Taken together, the work of the NGOs in the Caribbean Basin has contributed, firstly to the creation of transnational links and a regional awareness that helps overcome existing barriers; and secondly to a regional debate on development strategies and alternative projects, based on criticisms of the economic adjustment programmes and development strategies implemented in the 1980s. This climate is working in favour of the mobilisation and organisation of popular sectors by the emerging social movements, such as women's initiatives and the proposals for sustainable development proposed by the environmentalists, which are seen as a set of alternative projects to the growth model based on export led growth and free trade linked to the neoliberal views supported by the local political elite.

Moreover the movements and groups involved with human rights, peace and disarmament and social justice in the region have frequently been associated with these alternative projects. There is an active interaction between all these non-governmental organisations and the issues and projects they promote, in which the demands of women and the informal sector are associated with the defence of human rights, sustainable development as an alternative strategy and the promotion of regional peace and disarmament[23]. These alternative proposals are frequently backed by new networks of academic relationships which identify with their aims and with a regional view, in the framework of growing linkages between initiatives by non-governmental and popular organisations and those proposed by professional and university associations.

The academic network and the emerging epistemic community

Although historically area studies and its related academic networks in the Caribbean began to develop in the 1950s (Serbin, 1987) predominantly in the non-Hispanic area, the situation has been progressively changing to the point where academics and researchers from the insular Hispanic and the continental areas are becoming increasingly involved. Numerous regional academic organisations have contributed to this process, including UNICA, the Caribbean Studies Association (CSA), Coordinadora Regional de Institutos de Investigaciónes Económicas y Sociales (CRIES), the Association of Caribbean Economists (ACE) and the Working Group on International Relations in the Caribbean Basin of the Latin American Council of Social Sciences (CLACSO).

UNICA was founded in 1968 'as an inter-cultural hybrid of the Caribbean region which groups state and non-state research and higher educational institutions from the English-, Spanish-, French-, and Dutch-speaking areas' (Latorre, 1982, 3), with an initial representation from sixteen regional universities. Its principal aim is to 'contribute to the development of the Caribbean through cooperation in the broad field of higher education', functioning as a catalyst and innovator, a factor of convergence, and a promoter of development (ibid.). An evaluation of UNICA in 1982 found that its role 'as nexus of communication in the Caribbean region has been exemplary'. It was present in nine countries of the region with the support of US and Canadian foundations and the Venezuelan government, among others (Buttedabl, 1983, 14)[24].

The CSA was founded in the early 1970s by academics interested in area studies from Puerto Rico, the English-speaking Caribbean and the US. The CSA groups researchers from regional research centres all over the Caribbean, rising above linguistic, cultural and political barriers – its three official languages are English, Spanish and French. Fundamentally the development of research centres, like the Institute of Caribbean Studies of the University of Puerto Rico and the Institute of Social and Economic Studies of the University of the West Indies, has made an important contribution to promoting regional studies in social sciences and to creating a climate for communication between Caribbean researchers and academics. Its regular academic publications include *Caribbean Studies* and *Social and Economic Studies* (Maingot, 1983b). The CSA celebrated its twentieth anniversary at its annual meeting in Curacao in May 1995, and continues to publish its informative *Caribbean Studies Newsletter* every quarter.

CRIES was founded in Nicaragua in the early 1980s with the aim of coordinating research in the Central American area. Despite its originally Central American character it has been gradually forging ties with academic centres and non-governmental organisations in the Hispanic and non-Hispanic insular Caribbean. However despite these contacts, during the 1980s, its orientation and the majority of its publications – for example, *Pensamiento propio*, a monthly journal – were published in Spanish for Central and South American readers. In 1991 the participation of a representative group from the Caribbean – predominantly Jamaicans, Dominicans and Puerto Ricans – was influential in the establishment of a regional office of CRIES in the Caribbean, based in Santo Domingo in conjunction with the ACE (CRIES, 1992). CRIES along with the ACE, has close links with the NGOs in the Caribbean Basin, in terms of promoting alternative economic strategies through a network of political parties, popular organisations, and the scientific-intellectual community (CRIES, 1991, 16). Still the regional view of CRIES was more restricted and, until 1996, it expressly excluded from its board of directors, representatives of continental Latin American countries, principally Venezuela, Mexico and Colombia (CRIES, 1992).

The ACE has been bringing economists and social scientists together from all the linguistic areas of the insular and continental Caribbean since 1987. The ACE has produced a series of collective works, which offer a diagnosis of the economic situation of the countries of the region, based on the papers presented at its biannual meetings. These meetings have usually been held in the insular Caribbean, with the participation of economists and social scientists from the different linguistic areas. The range of topics dealt with stresses economic and development studies, with frequent comparative contributions.

Finally the Working Group on International Relations of the Caribbean Basin was created under the auspices of the Research

Centre of the University of Puerto Rico in 1988 and CLACSO, based in Buenos Aires. Its participants are predominantly from the insular Hispanic Caribbean – including a large Cuban representation – and continental Latin American countries – with a strong representation of Venezuelan and Mexican researchers. Its biannual meetings have been held in San Juan, Caracas, Cancun, the Virgin Islands and Aruba. Its general coordinators are appointed by CLACSO. This group has not yet published any collective material, other than the Puerto Rican material edited by the Centre of Social Research of the University of Puerto Rico. The general theme of the meetings is regional relations, focused from different viewpoints with an emphasis on decolonisation and regional integration.

This brief survey of academic networks would not be complete without mention of some of the regional research institutes and centres, and national associations, which have strengthened the networks by breaking down linguistic and cultural barriers and promoting studies on the region at subregional and national level (Serbin, 1994a and 1994b). Examples are the Centro de Estudios de América (CEA) of Havana; the Facultad Latinoamericana de Ciencias Sociales (FLACSO), a Dominican Republic programme; the Instituto Venezolano de Estudios Sociales y Políticos (INVESP); the Asociación Venezolana de Estudios Caribeños (AVECA) created in 1978, and the recently established Asociación Mexicana de Estudios Caribeños.

By way of preliminary conclusion

In the general context of the development of the network of non-governmental organisations in the Caribbean, interpenetration among the region's societies and interaction among non-governmental actors has been increasing, resulting in a much broader, more complex and structured regional agenda (Tomassini, 1989, 25). This is a consequence of the initiatives and interests, of a growing number of actors, that have formed a dense web of transnational relations, spaces and circuits for transnational interaction and issues of regional importance, stemming from the development of civil society. This process has not taken place in isolation from the effects of global changes or from the action of extra-regional governmental or non-governmental actors inherent in the globalisation process (Buzan, 1991). Its evolution is associated with the emergence of a regional view that is broader than that imposed by colonial legacies and compartmentalisation, in terms of the growing convergence of the interests of regional actors at both governmental and social levels.

This regional view is no longer confined to specific sectors of the governmental, political, economic and intellectual elite but has expanded and become more complex by the entry of new actors and by the spread of transnational relations among the civil societies of the Caribbean Basin, creating a broader perception of what the region is and what its priority interests are in the new international context. The development of this regional view seems, at first sight, to throw doubt on state-centred views and even on the role of the state and government in the regionalisation process in the context of the structuring of a previously non-existent *social community*. Non-governmental activities and alternative projects are proliferating as options to state strategies, stemming from the initiatives of the new social, religious and cultural movements, and from changes in the attitude of the private sector and the academic networks. This process is progressively generating, through a relational dynamic, an emergent regional civil society and a regionalisation process *from below*.

Nevertheless the development of transnational relations in the Caribbean Basin and the momentum acquired by a regional view promoted by a broad spectrum of actors, with possible clashes and divergences between the various projects and interests, is taking place in the framework of the general initiatives and strategies promoted domestically and regionally by governments. This general framework provides a specific context for the recent development of transnational relations, springing from the action of non-governmental actors which are increasingly factors of pressure for the continuity, reorientation or questioning of these initiatives and strategies.

It is difficult to predict what the scenarios for the region are in terms of integration and the deepening of the regional process, more so bearing in mind the decisive influence of exogenous factors. However in terms of the preceding survey, it is possible to conclude that a new broader and more complex regional vision is emerging, based on the development of a *social community* where the views generated by the different interests and projects combine, either antagonistically or harmoniously, to create a new regional network of transnational relations which transcends the fragmentation that has historically characterised the Caribbean Basin. To be effective in a heterogeneous and highly fragmented region, any initiative tending to deepen the regional integration process – such as the creation of the ACS – requires government action together with the consolidation and strengthening of a social and institutional network of the civil actors in the region, which is a prerequisite for integration based on wider social participation. An effective regional integration process, with the full participation of all the actors, can only emerge from the linking and convergence of the two processes.

There is no doubt that the growing links and interdependence between grass roots movements, religious and cultural groups, women's organisations, environmental and human rights movements and academic networks have been intensifying regional awareness and creating alternatives to the projects promoted by the dominant elite (Lewis, 1994). Regionalisation, in this sense, involves certain societal dimensions in terms of the creation of a network of social and political organisations to promote increased regional awareness. Yet the ACS does not intend to recognise these *social actors*, beyond a general reference in its constitutive convention. Recognition would be subject to a decision of the council of ministers[25].

According to the recommendations of the West Indian Committee (WIC), the ACS could, in principle, create a regional assembly or parliament (WIC, 1992), possibly along the lines of the EU, implicitly establishing integration goals that go beyond the formation of a free trade zone in the Caribbean Basin. However, although such a body could partially offset the *democratic deficit* in the regionalisation process, it would restrict political representation to the political parties. However a parliament would not open spaces for the representation and participation of the other groups, organisations and movements emerging in civil society which are increasingly committed to a regional view, though not necessarily the one promoted by the existing political and economic elite. It is paradoxical in this context that, despite attempts to reactivate the networks of the political parties in the region – at least in the case of the Christian and Social Democrats – there is no real debate or meaningful inclusion in their agendas of the effect of the globalisation process on regional integration and identity, or of democratic participation in the process.

We have also noted that this process creates a marked difference in the regional identifications assumed by social and political movements and organisations, and a growing differentiation from the political organisations that articulate traditional interests – principally the political parties and the trade unions. The parties are much weakened by the decline in the distributive capacity of the state and the system of political patronage that depends on it; and the unions by economic restructuring. The decline of these traditional political organisations – affected not only by the downsizing of the state but also by a growing perception of their involvement in corruption – has led to the emergence and proliferation of social movements and organisations that articulate the sectorial interests of groups, deprived of formal political representation, in the form of specific demands strongly identified with cultural, gender, ethnic and religious interests (Deere, 1990; Lewis, 1991).

The absence of links between these movements and the institutional channels of political representation and aggregation of interests, besides promoting a *transnationalised civil society* or a regional *social community*, can increase social and political fragmentation in terms of the formulation of alternative political projects or the necessary construction of consensus in the framework of pluralist democracies.

Fragmentation, however, can be an enriching experience for a democratic and pluralist, social and political dynamic if it develops in the framework of institutionalised systems of participation in decision making and in the context of the identification of a series of shared values and interests in the regional framework. On the other hand, taken to extremes and without an appropriate participative framework, the result can be the emergence of fundamentalist – rather than ideological in the present context – expressions of an ethnic or gender character. This fragmentation is also found in the first of the processes mentioned – the diversity of identifications and conceptualisations of the region promoted by these movements.

However, the regionalisation process, with its specific subtleties and differences, is not circumscribed to intergovernmental processes and free trade agreements promoted by the political and economic elite, but is under growing pressure from civil society, expressed in regional events of cultural and historical identification in which academic and cultural organisations play a significant part.

Notes

1 Based on the articles *Towards an Association of Caribbean States: Raising Some Awkward Questions*, Journal of Interamerican Studies and World Affairs, 1994, Vol. 36, No. 4; *¿Una reconfiguración de la Cuenca del Caribe?*, Nueva Sociedad, No. 133, September-October 1994; and *Integración y relaciones transnacionales: el entramado social de los procesos de regionalización en la Cuenca del Caribe*, in Perfiles Latinoamericanos (Mexico-FLACSO), Year 3, No. 4, June 1994.
2 The *wider view* responds to the Bourne Report's recommendations to the 1989 CARICOM meeting and to those of the West Indian Commission in 1992 (cf. Serbin, A., 1994d).
3 We have analysed elsewhere how the inclusion of Cuba creates a series of problems with the US, the principal interlocutor of the ACS (Serbin, A., 1994d).
4 Preparatory documentation (ACS, 1994a).

5　Following their participation in the Lomé Agreement with the EU at the beginning of this decade, the Dominican Republic and Haiti formed a specific forum, known as CARIFORUM with the member states of CARICOM. Suriname and Haiti have been recently admitted to membership of CARICOM.

6　This position was made evident, for example by the Trinidad and Tobago and the Guyana representatives, during the Havana ACS Ministerial Summit in December 1996.

7　The debate on the need to broaden the process of integration of CARICOM to the entire region because of the challenges imposed by the process of economic globalisation in reality dates back, in the context of the English-speaking Caribbean, to the presentation of the Bourne Report in 1988 and the Declaration of Gran Anse by the CARICOM heads of government in 1989. (See Lewis, 1995.)

8　The document also states that 'The rationale underlying this perception is advocated to repose on the fact that this enlarged regional space would provide a wider productive base, greater degrees of competitiveness, enhanced negotiating strength and a host of related advantages which could never accrue to nation states acting individually' (CARICOM, 1993, 2).

9　As already mentioned, following their incorporation in the Lomé Agreement, Haiti and the Dominican Republic joined with the CARICOM member states to form CARIFORUM – a consultative and coordinating body of the Caribbean countries linked to the agreement.

10　Although they joined the Group of Rio at the beginning of the 1990s thanks to the mediation of the Group of Three, their representation is limited to one spokesman for each subregion. Their limited influence – and presence – in the Group of Rio tends to be diluted even further by the priorities of the larger countries of Latin America.

11　These frictions were resolved with the choice of Port of Spain as the site of the ACS Secretariat and the election, at the summit meeting held in August 1995, of the Venezuelan Simón Molina Duarte as ACS Secretary. Even so tensions have persisted concerning the allocation of quotas for the operation of the secretariat, its composition and its level of political, financial and administrative authority, which were in evidence in the ministerial meeting in Guatemala in November of the same year.

12　This committee's activities in the early 1980s, especially in relation to the critical situation in Central America, resulted in the participation of the following parties as full members at the XVI Congress of the IS in Albufeiras (Portugal) in April 1983 – Barbados Labour Party (BLP); Partido de Liberación Nacional (PLN) of Costa Rica; Partido Revolucionario Dominicano (PRD); Movimiento Nacional Revolucionario (MNR) of El Salvador; New Jewel Movement of Grenada; Partido Socialista Democrático of Guatemala; Working People's Alliance of Guyana; People's National Party of Jamaica; Partido Independentista of Puerto Rico; St Lucia Progressive Labour Party and Acción Democrática of Venezuela, to mention only the parties from the Caribbean Basin (Williams, 1984, 305–10). Also attending as observers were Rasambleman Demokrat Nasyonal Progresis Ayisyen (RDNP), Union des Forces Patriotiques et Democratiques Haitiennes (IFOPADA) and Partido Revolucionario Institucional (PRI) of Mexico which led to the admission of the Permanent Commission of Latin American Political Parties (COPPPAL) as an observer with the International Socialist (ibid.).

13　The Friederich Ebert Stiftung, linked to the SPD of Germany, also played an important role in fostering activities at regional level to promote projects with a social-democratic content, especially in the trade union and political and economic areas.

In the 1970s and 1980s, this organisation had branches in Venezuela, Colombia and Mexico, as well as in Jamaica, Costa Rica and the Dominican Republic.
14 In this framework, Latin American parties such as APRA of Peru, PRI, Acción Democrática (AD) and the Movimiento Electoral del Pueblo (MEP) of Venezuela, Partido Justicialista (PJ) and Partido Socialista Popular (PSP) of Argentina, Partido Socialista (PS) of Chile and the Movimiento de Izquierda Revolucionaria (MIR) of Bolivia are joined by MEP de Aruba, People's United Party (PUP) of Belize, Dominica Labour Party, Konakom and Panpra of Haiti, People's National Party (PNP) of Jamaica, Partido Independentista Puertorriqueño (PIP) of Puerto Rico and St Lucia Labour Party. In 1991 Movimiento Lavalas of President Aristide of Haiti applied to join the Commission (COPPPAL, 1992b). In this framework of joint participation of parties from Hispanic America and the non-Hispanic Caribbean in the COPPPAL, a Caribbean Commission headed by PIP of Puerto Rico was formed in San Juan, Puerto Rico in April 1990 which has closely followed political events in Haiti, as well as in Suriname and Cuba (COPPPAL, 1992a).
15 Through this link Christian-democrat influence has been gradually widening to cover the entire non-Hispanic Caribbean. Now ODCA members include Dominica Freedom Party and St Kitts People's Action Movement, and as observers Anguilla National Alliance, People's Liberation Movement of Montserrat, United Worker's Party of St Lucia, New Democratic Party of St Vincent, Antigua Labour Party, Nevis Reformation Party and New National Party of Grenada. Other full members include Partido Demócrata Cristiano of Cuba – in exile, RDNP of Haiti, Partido Reformista of Dominican Republic, Partido Social-Cristiano COPEI of Venezuela. More recently United National Party of Trinidad – led by Basdeo Panday – established links with the organisation.
16 'Although the private sector recognises the urgency of completing the Caribbean integration process so as to compete in a world of trading blocks, many delegates remained concerned at the apparent inability of governments, and in particular their bureaucracies, to safeguard the position of the Caribbean in the new world order' (*CA*, 1992d, 2).
17 The seventh conference, held in Port of Spain, Trinidad in November 1995, focused on the changes in the policies of the EU on Latin America and the Caribbean. It is interesting to note how, in the case of the Caribbean Council for Europe, the agenda no longer centres solely on the Caribbean but increasingly associates the region with Latin America, as a result of a similar change in direction in EU cooperation and assistance policies and of uncertainty about the survival of the ACP Group (Africa, Caribbean and Pacific) of European ex-colonies that are the beneficiaries of Lomé.
18 The C/LAA is defined as 'a non-governmental non-profit organization formed in 1980 to help the countries of the Caribbean and Central America achieve their economic development goals through the resources of the private sector. C/LAA stimulates trade and investment, fosters responsible private-sector leadership in the region and promotes helpful public policies' (*CA*, 1991, 2). The most recent meeting of this group was held in Miami in December 1995 with the customary participation of businessmen and officials from governmental and inter-governmental agencies. MERCOSUR was one of the subjects on the agenda.
19 As the author states, 'Four factors have undermined the ability of organised labour to become effective mobilisers of popular discontent: the traditional umbilical cord between the unions and the parties throughout much of the Caribbean; the effective penetration of much of the labour movement by pro-capital U.S. institutions;

the lack of unions in sectors where the growing number of women workers are employed; and the inability to organise effectively in the informal sector' (Deere, 1990, 97).

20 This activity is well illustrated by the *Caribbean Encounter* held in May and June 1991 in Haiti which dealt with issues concerning the Caribbean's common history and identity, the popular struggles and the future of the region. Participants included the Centro Dominicano de Estudios de la Educación (CEDEE); Pastoral Haitiana Iglesia Episcopal; Servicio Social de Iglesias; Group of Interdenominational Pastors; the CCC; Centro Comunal de Guarenas of Venezuela; Comité Evangélico Venezolano para la Justicia; Programa Abierto para la Capacitación Teológica; Consejo Latinoamericano de Iglesias Regional; Presencia Cristiana Popular Paz Presente; Proyecto Caribeño Justicia y Paz of Puerto Rico; Misión Industrial and Fondo Ecuménico para el Desarrollo also of Puerto Rico; Service Chretien de Haiti; and other similar organisations from the English-, Spanish-, and French-speaking Caribbean (*Hoja CEDEE*, 1991, 7).

21 The situation in Central America seems to differ from that of the insular Caribbean, since De la Ossa (1996) mentions in a recent work the difficulties the ICIC (Iniciativa Civil para la Integración Latinoamericana) has encountered in promoting its positions at government level, despite the launch of the Alianza Centroamericana para el Desarrollo Sostenible in 1994 (*PC*, 1995a).

22 Examples are the Encuentro Internacional del Mundo del Caribe, organised in Caracas in November 1991 by the Consejo Nacional de la Cultura (CONAC), with participation by the countries of the insular and non-Hispanic Caribbean, and the festivals of Caribbean culture regularly sponsored by the Casa del Caribe de Santiago de Cuba (*CONAC*, 1991; *Festival del Caribe*, 1993).

23 In March 1989, under the auspices of CARIPEDA and OXFAM America, a meeting of NGOs was held to analyse the impact of the programmes of USAID, the World Bank and the International Monetary Fund. The meeting was attended by CARIPEDA, CCC, WAND, CAFRA, Windward Islands Farmers Association (WINFA), Eastern Caribbean Popular Theatre Organization (ECPTO); Projects Promotion (St Vincent and the Grenadines); Small Projects Assistance Team (SPAT, Dominica); Development Alternatives (Dominica); Association for Rural Transformation (ART, Grenada); Grenada Community Development Agency (GRENCODA); Association of Development Agencies (ADA, Jamaica); Projects for People (Jamaica); Folk Research Center (St Lucia); Action Committee of Women Against Free Trade Zones (Trinidad and Tobago); Belize Agency for Rural Development (BARD); Grenada Cane Farmers Association; GRENSAVE (Grenada); Grenada Fruit and Nutrition Corporation; Caribbean Branch of the Canadian University Service Organisation (CUSO); InterPares (Canada); The Development Gap (USA) and OXFAM America (McAfee, 1991, 10).

24 Another report makes the following comments on the activities of the organisation; 'Perhaps the greatest strength of UNICA is its independence – its freedom of operation. It selects its own leadership, determine its own policies, manages its own affairs. UNICA having no political ideology is free to draw on a wide range of Caribbean expertise. Having no bureaucracy, it enjoys flexibility and freedom to act quickly and directly. It represents a rich mix of people and talents. It provides a unique Caribbean resource of scholarship and expertise, as well as institutional facilities ... It is perhaps the only one truly academic organization in the Caribbean. It is legitimately organised as a Caribbean institution and provides a way for building the much needed linkages between the Spanish and the non-Spanish speaking Caribbean' (Weelhausen, 1984, 25).

25 It is interesting to note that the English version of the ACS Constitutive Agreement uses the term *social partners* while the Spanish version speaks of *actores sociales*, which would presumably include, without distinction, business associations, political parties and social movements. However the ACS ministerial meeting held in Guatemala in November 1995 approved, among other things, rules for the admission of social partners with special emphasis on regional academic institutions. Notwithstanding this decision the ACS Havana Summit, held in December 1996, postponed any decision on the inclusion of social partners as observers.

5 Towards an agenda for the Greater Caribbean – the exogenous and endogenous challenges

'Every exit is an entrance to some other place'
Tom Stoppard

The establishment and consolidation of the ACS and the regionalisation process stimulated *from above* and *from below* are all facing a series of specific challenges. Some of these challenges derive from the exogenous dynamic in the context of a global and hemispheric perspective, while others point to a set of factors related to an endogenous dynamic with its own characteristics, questions and problematic nuclei. The linking of both dynamics – the global and the regional – rather than imposing a unified, uniform process on regionalisation generates new ruptures and conflicts, or confers new modalities on old ones, in the framework of the evolution of the ACS and the intersocietal process developed by the emerging regional civil society. These ruptures and contradictions help to identify the specific challenges that these processes face, sometimes overcoming and at other times reactivating the region's old fragmentations and cleavages, under pressure from new factors and variables, in the context of the interaction between the global and regional dynamic, without disregarding the weight of the domestic dynamic. Yet as we said in the introduction, for the purpose of this book, we prefer to focus on the regionalisation and transnationalisation resulting from the impact of global relations and processes, while assuming a close and growing interdependence between the international and domestic spheres.

As Hurrell and Wood (1995) rightly point out, the globalisation process is deeply affected by the inequalities between states, regions and non-state actors. The strength and capacity of the states, marked by the strength of domestic governments, has a significant effect on their capacity to adapt to and obtain benefits from globalisation, with devastating effects for small and vulnerable states such as the majority of Caribbean and Central American countries. The alternatives for dealing with this inequality through apparently neutral international and regional institutions that oversee interdependence, such as the ACS, clash with the reality that these institutions are frequently the stage where the power and influence of states is wielded and where the rules are generally imposed by the most powerful and influential. These inequalities need to be redressed by clear consensual rules – not at all easy to negotiate or establish.

The inequality between regions and the traditional *peripheralisation* of the Greater Caribbean requires clear strategies and rules for interaction with the centres of world economic dynamism. In this perspective the inequalities among the states of a region have to be reduced in the interests of an effective regional strategy designed to improve positioning in relations with the more important international actors; coordinate efforts and actions; and make possible effective concerted political action. In this respect the institutionalisation of a forum and regional platform is a fundamental mechanism for integration into the global context from the economic, political and social point of view. Hence the need for a broad regional strategy that covers all the components of the regional system, and which transcends existing inequalities.

Likewise the emergence of a transnational civil society under the impact of globalisation does not escape these inequalities. Clear differences are discernible between the power and influence of the NGOs from industrialised countries and those from the Third World. These differences apply equally to the well intentioned NGOs that express the interests of diverse social movements and groups, and those linked to transnational terrorism or criminality, including both groups that are politically representative and those that question all legitimacy, representation and democratic political participation (Hurrell and Wood, 1995, 468–70). As a result the emerging regional civil society is not in itself a defined actor but rather a context in which a large number of groups (Shaw, 1994, 648) struggle to impose their hegemony and their interests, and resist the attempts of other actors to impose theirs.

It is on the basis of these and other inequalities and differences that we will try to identify the main challenges facing the Greater Caribbean, in an international setting transformed by a series of recent global processes. However these processes are often anchored to dissimilar legacies which make significant differences in the regional context; to new fissures that are emerging in the regional dynamic; and to the confusion of contradictory discourses and narratives under the apparent hegemony of the neoliberal discourse.

The challenge of globalisation – reconfiguration, competitive integration and security

As we concluded earlier, the dynamic of economic globalisation revolves around four fundamental factors that are producing a clear reconfiguration and a series of specific challenges for the region. These four factors, (1) financial globalisation; (2) global restructuring of production; (3) the underlying technical-scientific revolution – especially advances in information technology; and (4) growing trade liberalisation and interdependence; are prompting the configuration of a global dynamic of the international economic system with new characteristics. Taken together globalisation of production and trade, and the focusing of economic and technical-scientific dynamism in the economic-political blocs – of North America, the EU, Japan and Southeast Asia – create a clear challenge in terms of the integration – particularly competitive integration – of the region in the international economic system.

For a region used to playing the so-called 'Cuban card' in the context of the Cold War, and to obtaining economic and technical assistance and cooperation from the former European metropolises (Lomé Convention and San Jose dialogue), and from the US and Canada through the ICC and CARIBCAN, the dilution of the strategic importance of the Caribbean has meant redirecting its strategies for development and economic growth, and a reconfiguration of the region and its limits. Under pressure from the search for a more competitive integration into the international economy, the majority of regional states have realised the advantages of a regionalisation process based on a broader concept of integration, which embraces the insular countries of the Caribbean Sea along with the continental countries of the Caribbean Basin.

The very small economic spaces of the domestic markets of some of the countries of the region require diversification; an increase in regional trade; and the establishment of forms of regional cooperation; in an effort to optimise the capacities of these vulnerable economies, marked by the exploitation of natural resources and reliance on a limited range of exports. This need has steered the ACS initiative toward a wider geographical framework, than CARICOM, the Central American scheme or the Group of Three, which has involved countries like Cuba and the Dominican Republic, previously outside the context of subregional schemes. However, the competitive integration of the Greater Caribbean, in the framework of the reconfiguration of the regional system in terms of cooperation and free trade, requires the development of regional strategies to compensate and reduce the asymmetries between ACS members, and to promote free trade. The scheme also requires a series of coordinated strategies to restructure production, reorient sectors of the economy, attract financial flows and foster technological modernisation, accompanied by a common regional policy oriented toward the traditional centres of world economic dynamism.

This process requires a major political effort to promote different forms of cooperation and coordination in a bid to reduce national friction, coupled with the involvement of an array of new regional transnational interlocutors, among them transnational corporations, multilateral and non-governmental organisations, and a group of new actors at regional, hemispheric and global level, characterised by unequal capacities of power, projection and influence in the regional and global system. Exclusions and pressures of different kinds deepen the inequalities imposed by the globalisation process. To counteract them a strong collective will is needed with explicit rules and procedures; a common identification; and solid, democratic and participative regional institutions. On this basis regional actors will be able to promote a beneficial and competitive integration into the international system, resulting in economic growth, sustainable development and social and political equity.

As we noted in Chapter 3, with the end of the Cold War, the regional security agenda has gradually shifted from external threats to transnational threats anchored in the domestic situation; from containment of Cuban-Soviet influence and territorial conflicts and disputes to control of terrorism, drug trafficking, immigration and transnational criminal activities. These problems are overwhelming the preventive capacity of governments in terms of social policies, intelligence and control of the financial activities generated by these phenomena, not to mention the institutions and human resources needed to maintain control – namely the military and police forces – with appropriate training, equipment and organisational structures. In this framework the challenge of security, in the new conditions imposed by globalisation, requires a reassessment of the traditional concepts of military threats. New elements have to be incorporated – socio-economic factors linked to social and development policies; socio-political factors related to human and legal rights at transnational level; and, most of all, financial aspects concerning the control of illegal flows of funds produced by or supporting illegal activities (Griffith, 1995; Griffith and Munroe, 1995).

Paradoxically the intergovernmental meetings held to create the ACS have not considered the traditional issues of security and control of drug trafficking has been mentioned only once – at the summit meeting in Port of Spain in August 1995.

The challenge of hemispheric polarisation

The establishment of a platform of regional political coordination through the ACS is also of special importance for meeting hemispheric and regional challenges. On the one hand, the decreasing impact of the centripetal dynamic of NAFTA – following the domestic political and economic obstacles in the US and the possible reticence of Canada and Mexico to expand the free trade area to other countries – makes the accession of the Caribbean Basin countries into the North American scheme an ever more distant objective, even though at the Miami Summit, Clinton's administration emphasised the goal of creating a hemispheric free trade area by 2005.

In spite of repeated assertions, by some analysts, that the Caribbean Basin's natural geographical and strategic conditions will ensure a smooth incorporation into NAFTA – reinforced by the fact that North America, especially the US, is the Caribbean's major trading partner – the region can expect increasing difficulties in gaining entry into NAFTA. Clear evidence of this is the US Congress's recent decision to deny Caribbean countries the same conditions of access to the US market as Mexico – the so-called 'parity' which would compensate, to some extent, for Mexican competition with certain Caribbean products – and the decline in assistance to the region (*CU*, 1995, 1–2).

Meanwhile in South America, the integrationist dynamic is beginning to revolve in political terms around the Group of Rio – in which the Caribbean and Central America have little participation – and in economic terms around ALADI and MERCOSUR – in which they have none. In the framework of the idea of a South American Free Trade Area (SAFTA), the Brazilian initiatives to promote the incorporation of Venezuela and Colombia, and eventually the Andean Pact, into a common scheme with MERCOSUR, are concentrating the Latin American integrationist dynamic in South America, particularly in the Southern Cone. This trend was recently reinforced by the association of Chile – which is also first in line for membership of NAFTA – with MERCOSUR, followed closely by Bolivia.

The hemispheric polarisation between the dynamics of North and South America has weakened the traditional pivotal role of the Caribbean Basin, posing dilemmas and challenges for integration at both global and hemispheric levels, in the context of the possible evolution of a Free Trade Area of the Americas, as proposed at the Miami Summit in December 1994. In this respect the particularities of economic asymmetry; the cultural and linguistic heterogeneities; inequalities of size; and the absence of a common historical experience; have created an important strategic challenge. The latter aspect could be overcome if extra-regional foreign policies based on a regional political platform were effectively coordinated within the ACS, in a situation in which both the US and the EU are tending to ignore the region. However without clearly identified strategies and effective coordinated action to meet the demands of globalisation, particularly in terms of trade, transportation and tourism – as stressed during the ACS Summit in Port of Spain – the regional challenges imposed by the global dynamic will not be easily transformed into linkages and a reduction of economic asymmetries and complementarities.

In particular a crucial challenge for the region is the goal of reorienting the majority of regional economies to trade in services – especially tourism; expanding and diversifying manufacturing capacity; and adopting the latest technological advances; to improve the region's competitive capacity in a wider economic space. This challenge requires the formulation of a clear coordinated strategy, based on the identification of the regional effects of short term demands and medium and long term global mega-trends.

The challenge of heterogeneity and regional fragmentation

However the possibilities of meeting these exogenous challenges through the regionalisation process in the Greater Caribbean is also hampered by the extremely heterogeneous character of the region, most evident in its cultural, linguistic and ethnic characteristics, but also in the diversity of political cultures and legal systems, asymmetries of economy and size, political status and the persistence of fragmentations and cleavages of different kinds. The path to regionalisation is made more difficult by the distinctive cultural, legal and ethnic legacies in the four linguistic areas that form the Caribbean Basin; the fragmentations in its diverse conceptualisations; the difficulties inherent in the creation of a common identity beyond the territorial limits of each state; the heterogeneity of political systems and cultures and constitutional and legal frameworks; all of which is exacerbated by differences in size, potential, economic development and availability of resources.

A good illustration is Cuba's admission into the ACS. In the geopolitical sphere it could affect the ACS's relations with the US; economically, it could speed up Cuba's transition to a market economy and its competitive integration into the regional dynamic; while politically, the island's different political system and culture could be a source of regional tension. A similar illustration, despite differences in distance and size, is provided by the inclusion – as associated members or observers – of the British and Dutch associated states and territories and the French overseas departments. Their status in the ACS is likely to be a source of ambiguities. Great Britain and Holland hope that by joining an economically-based regional scheme, their associated states will become progressively disassociated from the metropolis, thus releasing them from their commitments in the region, which are no longer of strategic importance. In contrast France has directly assumed the representation of its overseas departments as an associated member of the ACS, despite the country's extra-regional character. As a result France became an actor in the organisation, maintaining the strategic importance of its territories long after the end of the Cold War (Serbin, 1989a).

These two examples illustrate some of the aspects of the challenge that heterogeneity imposes on the region and the need to introduce innovative mechanisms and processes to successfully deal with it. However in addition to these specific situations, the region's major challenge is the heterogeneity and superposition of subregional schemes, in terms of the speed of integration, divergence of interests and institutional duplication due to the presence of the three schemes already mentioned – CARICOM, the Central American integration process and the evolution of the G-3 free trade agreement. Although the proposal for a *wider view* of the Greater Caribbean basically springs from within CARICOM, a special effort of political will is required to coordinate and harmonise the interests of the three schemes, in terms of dissimilar expectations and the speed of subregional integration.

This problem is aggravated by the difficulty of overcoming the historical separation – and the resulting friction – between the countries of the English-speaking Caribbean and Central America, recently marked by the trade dispute over banana exports to Europe, and by differing expectations and speeds of integration with NAFTA and Mexico. Moreover the uncertainties in the progress of the G-3 free trade agreement and the difficult domestic situations in the three member countries, are reflected in the tensions and friction over regional and hemispheric priorities and objectives which are preventing a more active involvement in the ACS, despite these countries' historical commitment to the region. To this panorama has to be added the need to reconcile the interests of countries such as the Dominican Republic, Haiti and Cuba – not associated with any of the subregional schemes but member of the ACS – and the states and territories associated with the EU and the US. The result is a complex challenge arising from the heterogeneity and historical fragmentation of the Greater Caribbean.

The political challenges of sovereignty, participation and representation

The regionalisation process advanced by the ACS is also leading to the emergence of very specific challenges at the political and social level, basically in relation to the redefinition of the scope of the external and internal sovereignty of the states. In this respect the pressure for the partial transfer of sovereignty in the framework of regionalisation involves a difficult reassessment for countries that are emerging from a stage of strong reaffirmation of their national sovereignty and self determination in the aftermath of the decolonisation process, in a context where geographical and territorial limitations and the fragile consolidation of their distinctive political cultures are affecting the formation of clearly structured national identities.

Although as we have seen, this process is taking place in terms of a loss of independence by the states through economic globalisation, in the Caribbean Basin it touches a sensitive nerve. Among other reasons, it is because the most recent phase of the process of consolidating the nation states has occurred in the context of the revindication of post-colonial self determination – with chronological differences between the Hispanic insular, non-Hispanic and continental Caribbean – without, in many cases, concluding in an effective consolidation of the nation state and its national identity. As Watson remarks, national sovereignty came late to the insular Caribbean in the context of its integration into the international state system (Watson, 1994c, 5). Moreover the process has involved an identification with a national sovereignty equivalent to that of the nation states formed earlier in the North Atlantic, despite differences in size and economic and demographic potentialities. Thus the mere mention of a transfer of sovereignty even in terms of a gradual and partial regionalisation, frequently generates serious reluctance (Whiting, 1993, 3)[1].

An additional factor is that the transnationalisation of civil societies and the multiplication of non-governmental regional actors is complicating the scope of the domestic policies of the states and their regional projection, at the same time as requiring new forms of political expression and participation for a wide range of social actors, some of which clearly benefit from economic regionalisation and the adjustment programmes, while others suffer their more perverse effects.

The political challenge of regionalisation has two dimensions. The first relates to the transfer of national sovereignty in order to move forward with regional integration, through linkage with, and subordination to, coordinating schemes and regional rules, frequently at the cost of rescaling the traditional capacity and function of a nation state in the international sphere. This challenge requires clear but flexible rules for regionalisation, the formulation of appropriate mechanisms to overcome possible conflicts, and the constitution of legal schemes and institutions to regulate and strengthen them. While not questioning the essential functions of the nation state – subject to increasing reassessment and much criticised in its traditional overgrown form – the process does require a redefinition and a creative rescaling of its functions of state, which some social and political actors are resisting in favour of their own interests. It also requires decisions at intergovernmental level through appropriate and innovative mechanisms, in terms of the medium and long term consolidation of the regionalisation process.

The second dimension is the transnationalisation of civil society and the multiplication of social and political actors, whose actions exceed the territorial limits of the states and who frequently postulate demands of a regional character, creating a series of challenges to the state in its domestic dimension and regional linkages. Although some analysts like Drainville consider that in the 'new world order, there are no citizens of the world economy, only national citizens in the world economy' (Drainville, 1995, 60) because of the non-existence of mechanisms of individual participation in the globalisation process, this contradiction is leading to strong pressure for the establishment of citizens' rights at transnational level and the emergence of regional movements from civil society.

Increasingly the citizens of a country tend to be identified with a national and possibly regional and global citizenship, as a result of the claims and demands associated with regional or global issues – ranging from environmental protection to ethnic and gender issues. In this context, new forms of citizenship are based on three central propositions, (1) equality with respect to human and individual rights; (2) free and universal political participation; and (3) state responsibility for adequate levels of human wellbeing (UNRISD – United Nations Research Institute for Social Development, 1995, xxiii). These demands create new challenges in terms of individual rights and mechanisms of participation.

We have mentioned the absence of provisions for mechanisms of citizen participation, in the regionalisation process promoted by the ACS, which runs counter to the growing aspirations of a broad spectrum of social actors. Many of these actors are seeking an active part in the decision making processes that affect their daily lives, particularly in the context of the globalisation of democracy as a form of political participation, with evident effects on representation and legitimisation, not to mention governability. Nevertheless, there is a clear socio-political difficulty in overcoming the *democratic deficit* that all integration brings with it and which, as we remarked earlier, is particularly evident in the regionalisation process in the Caribbean, and can be expressed in terms of the principle 'we will decide for you, about you, but without you'.

This difficulty is clearly illustrated in the case of the EU, which is the integration scheme that has made most progress toward the formation of a *social community* and institutionalised mechanisms of political participation. Even so the democratic deficit is particularly evident in the role of the European Parliament and in the absence of mechanisms of participation for civil society[2]. Likewise negotiations for free trade agreements frequently ignore the socio-political effects of the schemes and especially their social consequences in terms of equity and specific policies aimed at participation and representation, as the NAFTA case illustrates. As a result one of the most decisive challenges of the regionalisation process is to devise creative mechanisms of participation and political expression at regional level in which the boundaries between domestic and international issues are diluted and diffused, particularly in the economic-political sphere. Their introduction is facilitated by the exhaustion of the traditional mechanisms of political expression – political parties, unions and possibly parliaments and legislatures associated with the redefinition of the social welfare state and populist political systems.

If they are to be successful, the processes of regionalisation and integration must include the creation of institutions and legal frameworks that stimulate more active social participation in decision making on the objectives of the process, its stages and the interests to which it responds. It is particularly important to ensure that the sensitivities aroused by the transfer of sovereignty are not channelled into fundamentalist responses, under the cloak of cultural demands, which would create more fragmentation and *globalitarian* temptations (Rogalski, 1994) in the bureaucratic sectors. It is imperative to develop democratic and pluralist institutionalised mechanisms, in the framework of the regionalisation process, which could eventually embrace a broad range of regional institutions – from regional parliaments and forums to consultative modalities and mechanisms with business, trade unions and non-governmental organisations.

These observations provoke critical questions on regionalisation in the Greater Caribbean as a response to the challenges of globalisation. Short term, immediate responses in *globalitarian* terms by the regional elite can only lead in the medium and long run to new frustrations and stagnation in the regional integration process. On the other hand, broader and more participative debates and responses can, through the development of institutionalised regional mechanisms, bring about more pluralist and democratic commitments with respect to their urgency and future. First, however, these questions have to be placed on the regional agenda, with the clear intention of promoting common views, building consensus and identity, and stimulating convergent projects in a region characterised by heterogeneity and growing complexity.

The social challenges – equity, employment, consumption and citizenship

Paradoxically the emergence of a regional or global citizenship is not disassociated from the phenomenon of growing political, economic and social marginalisation and deprivation of broad sectors of the population, particularly due to the effects of the economic adjustment programmes that sustain trade liberalisation and the export-oriented development strategies associated with the creation of spaces of regional integration. The redirection of strategies for economic growth and the emphasis on the correction of macroeconomic imbalances, aside from its effects on social equity, has increased unemployment, particularly in the unskilled work force and informal sectors. The priority assigned to economic policies associated with the adjustment programmes, to the detriment of social considerations, has reinforced this trend in most of the countries of the Caribbean and in Latin America in general.

The processes of streamlining production, introducing technological innovation and reorienting the economy towards trade in services, which requires an increase in highly skilled manpower, are hurting the sectors that traditionally provide unskilled manpower by limiting the supply of jobs. Consequently levels of poverty and unemployment are rising, principally among women, youth and the rural population (UN ECLAC/CDCC, 1994, 11).

Paradoxically these sectors and the population as a whole are increasingly exposed to information on patterns of consumption through mass access to the media and the associated entertainment industries, in the context of the technological and information expansion associated with the globalisation process. This promotion of values, expectations and habits of consumption more appropriate to the industrialised societies, is especially evident in the English-speaking Caribbean because of its geographical and linguistic proximity to the US, but it is also apparent in the Caribbean's other linguistic areas (Brown, 1995, 49).

García Canclini notes that under the effects of the logic of the market and the impact of mass communication 'some consumers want to be citizens' (García Canclini, 1995, 54). However, income distribution in the countries of the region – and in many others – under the effects of the adjustment programmes, is becoming increasingly inequitable. Broad sectors of the population are being marginalised from the conspicuous consumption promoted by globalisation, and simultaneously from the capacity to express themselves politically as citizens. At an increasing rate, 'people's possibilities of improving their lives are being fundamentally affected by decisions taken in international forums (characterised by non-accountability to world society for their actions as well as by their low level of representativeness) and which permit global markets to wreak havoc on the means of livelihood of a great part of the world population' (UNRISD, 1995, xxii).

In this context the different forms of consumption, linked to the modalities of global consumption, produce characteristic expressions of group identity, through consumption or the expectations it generates. Global consumption also generates deprivation and exclusion which lead to political or psychological attitudes of rejection and questioning, or to patterns of anomie and frustration, frequently ignored or minimised by the elite that support the regional and global processes. In this context, the challenges of social equity and equitable access to the goods and values that define the quality of life for broad sectors of the population, are frequently associated with aspirations for a more participative role in politics at national, regional and global level.

The challenge of strengthening regional human resources – the creation of a regional epistemic community

On the whole analytical enumeration, of the challenges confronting the Greater Caribbean in dealing with the processes of globalisation and regionalisation at the economic, social, political and cultural levels, creates uncertainties that can only really be solved by a political commitment on the part of the elite and a more participative system for the sectors affected. The urgent need to design and establish appropriate regional strategies to meet these challenges goes hand in hand with the challenge of strengthening human resources at regional level, in order to broaden, deepen and maximise the spectrum of possibilities for competitive integration through equitable and participative modalities in the globalisation process, as well as to optimise the capacity of the political and economic elite and the emerging regional civil society to respond to these challenges.

In this framework the development of a regional epistemic community – with the characteristics outlined in earlier chapters – could strengthen, through existing technological resources, a decentralised network of researchers and analysts who are able to provide regional decision makers with the inputs needed to deepen the regionalisation process and optimise the possibilities of competitive integration into the international system. Such a community also reaffirms, through regional interaction and cooperation, the distinctive characteristics of the identity of a Greater Caribbean faced by global challenges, on the basis of cultural and historical confluences and socio-political convergence rather than on coincidences in habits of consumption. As Haas notes, this development facilitates the circulation of ideas from society to government and among the countries of the region (Haas, 1992, 17), contributing to a dilution of traditional heterogeneity and fragmentation.

In this respect a crucial element, in any attempt to promote a regional view and action in responding to globalisation, is the strengthening and broadening of the critical mass created by the formation of a decentralised but strongly interactive regional epistemic community, based on individuals and regional and extra-regional institutions and centres. This community is able to debate its ideas and findings in regional forums and transmit them, through publications and other mechanisms of dissemination, to the principal interlocutors and actors in the regionalisation process[3].

The development of a regional epistemic community with these characteristics is an important mechanism for providing information and inputs for the region's political decision makers, and for spreading knowledge and awareness in a permanent interlocution with the actors in civil society. The combination of different values, technical know-how and capacity for a strategic perspective and interlocution with a broad spectrum of actors, can transform a regional epistemic network or community of this kind into a significant factor in the process of integration and regionalisation, by strengthening human resources beyond national borders.

Still in these times of globalisation, an epistemic community cannot and should not be disassociated, in the interests of a poorly understood regionalism, from advances in theoretical and practical knowledge made in other parts of the world. Mechanisms of information, connection, linkage and debate have to be established with researchers, centres and institutions outside the region.

By way of colophon

The advances towards regional integration, which were initiated by a series of economic and political determinations in the framework of the globalisation process, require short term responses based on improving regional competitiveness, expansion of regional economic spaces aimed at increasing intra-regional and extra-regional trade, and strategies for better integration in the international economic system. But these advances also create a series of challenges in the design of strategic responses to global and hemispheric change, and in the formulation of policies for citizen participation, and for improving the quality of life for broad sectors of the population in the medium and long term.

To achieve this, it is not enough simply to identify and debate the challenges; the political and economic elite and the different actors involved – including the participants in a regional epistemic network – have to develop a creative capacity and acquire the political will to create adaptable and participative institutions for the consolidation of an integration process that fully incorporates political and social dimensions and the aspirations of the population in general.

In addition to the political will, the promotion of agreements and forms of cooperation in an increasingly complex region and world, requires human resources with significant technical capacities which can only be achieved with coordinated training policies. In this respect focusing on specific objectives, without projecting them onto a broader perspective through structures, processes and actors at global, hemispheric, regional and domestic levels, restricts the capacity to meet these challenges in terms of a long term strategic vision. In the framework of the dynamism and complexity of international trade, of financial globalisation and technological development, the challenge of preparing human resources for globalisation is crucial, particularly for countries with a smaller critical mass and with meagre resources for development. Hence, the importance of strengthening regional resources, both material and human, to meet the challenges of globalisation in all its dimensions.

However, the broader debate – in regional and socio-political terms – which this book has attempted to develop, with all the distortions and limitations inherent in any individual effort, is also an effort to systematise some of the questions posed, order the uncertainties, and provoke, within the limits of a written text, a reflection on the destiny of the region, its future identity and its survival in a globalised world in a period of transition characterised by the absence of certainties and answers.

Notes

1 Parry identifies three kinds of response to the new conditions of interdependence – (1) 'the statist response', (2) 'the relative state sovereignty response' and (3) 'the cosmopolitan response' – in function of the diverse degrees of transfer of sovereignty by the states. In respect to (2) he states that 'it concedes more sovereignty and looks to some form of sustained institutionalised, supranational authority which can regulate those areas of policy which have been recognised as beyond the national capacity to organise and which also require more than intermittent negotiation' (Parry, 1994, 7–9).
2 See Neureither (1994) and Pinder (1994) on the democratic deficit in the EU.
3 The decision of the ACS ministerial meeting, held in Guatemala in November 1995, to incorporate regional academic institutions as recognised social actors, is an important step in this direction.

Bibliography

Albert, M. (1993) *Capitalismo contra capitalismo*, Buenos Aires, Paidós.
Allum, P. (1995) *State and Society in Western Europe*, Cambridge, Polity Press.
Anderson, B. (1983) *Imagined Communities*, London, Verso Press.
Augé M. (1994a) *Pour une anthropologie des mondes contemporaines*, Paris, Aubier.
Augé, M. (1994b) *Le sens des autres*, Paris, Fayard.
Badie, B. and Smouts, M. C. (1992) *Le retournement du monde. Sociologie de la scene internationale*, Paris, Presses de la Fondation Nationale des Sciences Politiques/Dalloz.
Balassa, B. (1980) *Teoría de la integración económica*, México, Uteha.
Banks, M. (ed.), (1988) *Conflict in World Society*, Sussex, Harvester Press.
Bansart, A. (ed.), (1989) *El Caribe: identidad cultural y desarrollo*, Caracas, Equinoccio.
Bartilow, H. (1997) *The Debt Dilemma – IMF Negotiations in Jamaica, Grenada and Guyana*, London, Macmillan.
Benitez Rojo, A. (1989) *La isla que se repite. El Caribe y la perspectiva postmoderna*, Hannover, Ediciones del Norte.
Baldwin, D. (ed.), (1993) *Neorealism and Neoliberalism: The Contemporary Debate*, New York, Columbia University Press.
Borges, J. L. (1974) 'Las ruinas circulares', *Obras Completas*, Buenos Aires, Emecé Editores.
Boxill, I. (1993) *Ideology and Caribbean Integration*, Mona, Consortium Graduate School of Social Sciences.
Brecher, J., Childs, J. B. and Cutler, J. (eds), (1993) *Global Visions. Beyond the New World Order*, Boston, South End Press.
Bryan, A. (ed.), (1995) *The Caribbean. New Dynamics in Trade and Political Economy*, Miami, North-South Center/New Brunswick, Transaction Publishers.
Bryan, A. and Serbin, A. (eds), (1996) *Distant Cousins. Latin American and Caribbean Relations*, Miami, North-South Center/New Brunswick, Transaction Publishers.
Bull, H. (1977) *The Anarchical Society*, Oxford, Oxford University Press.
Burton, J. and Dukes, F. (eds), (1990) *Conflict. Readings in Management and Resolution*, New York, Saint Martin's Press.
Burton, R. and Reno, F. (eds), (1995) *French and West Indian: Martinique, Guadeloupe and French Guiana Today*, London, Macmillan.
Camillieri, J. and Falk, J. (1992) *The End of Sovereignty? The Politics of a Shrinking and Fragmenting World*, Aldershot, Edward Elgar.
Campbell, D. (1992) *Writing Security: United States Foreign Policy and the Politics of Identity*, Minneapolis, University of Minnesota Press.
Carvajal, I. (1993) *Integración, pragmatismo y utopía en América Latina*, Bogotá, Universidad de los Andes/Universidad Externado de Colombia/Centro de Estudios Internacionales de la Universidad de los Andes.

CLADDE-FLACSO (1994) *El Caribe en la Postguerra Fría*, Santiago, CLADDE-FLACSO.
Club of Rome (1991) *The First Global Revolution*, London, Simon and Schuster.
Cohen, J. and Arato, A. (1992) *Civil Society and Political Theory*, Cambridge, Massachusetts Institute of Technology (MIT).
The Commission of Global Governance (1995) *Our Global Neighbourhood*, Oxford, Oxford University Press.
Cox, R. (1987) *Production, Power and World Order. Social Forces in the Making of History*, New York, Columbia University Press.
Dabydeen, D. and Samaroa, B. (eds), (1996) *Across the Dark Waters – Ethnicity and Indian Identity in the Caribbean*, London, Macmillan.
Deere, C. D. et al., (1990) *In the Shadows of the Sun. Caribbean Development Alternatives and the U.S.*, Boulder, Westview press/PACCA.
Der Derian, J. and Shapiro, M. J. (eds), (1989) *International/Intertextual Relations*, Lexington, Massachusetts/Lexington Books.
Deutsch, K. (1969) *Nationalism and its alternatives*, New York, Alfred Knopf.
Domínguez, J., Pastor, R. and Worrell, D. (eds), (1993) *Democracy in the Caribbean*, Baltimore, The Johns Hopkins University Press.
Dougherty, J. E. and Pfaltzgraff, R. L. (1990) *Contending Theories of International Relations*, New York, Harper and Row.
Escobar, A. and Alvarez, S. (eds), (1992) *The Making of Social Movements in Latin America. Identity, Strategy and Democracy*, Boulder, Westview.
Frankel, J. (1988) *International Relations in a Changing World*, Oxford, Oxford University Press.
Frohmann, A. (1990) *Puentes sobre la turbulencia. La concertación política latinoamericana en los ochenta*, Santiago de Chile, FLACSO.
Gamus, R. (1990) *Una fugaz convergencia: CAP y la I.S. en Centroamérica*, Caracas, Fondo Editorial Acta Científica.
García Canclini, N. (1995) *Consumidores y ciudadanos: conflictos multiculturales de la globalización*, Mexico, Grijalbo.
Giddens, A. (1993) *Consecuencias de la modernidad*, Madrid, Alianza.
Gilpin, R. (1987) *The Political Economy of International Relations*, Princeton, Princeton University Press.
Gill, S. and Law, D. (1988) *The Global Political Economy: Perspectives, Problems and Policies*, Baltimore, Johns Hopkins University Press.
Gleick, J. (1987) *Chaos. Making a New Science*, New York, Penguin Books.
Goldstein, J. and Keohane, R. O. (eds), (1993) *Ideas and Foreign Policy: Beliefs, Institutions and Political Change*, Ithaca, Cornell University Press.
Greene, J. and Scowcroft, B. (eds), (1985) *Intereses Occidentales y política de Estados Unidos en la Cuenca del Caribe*, Buenos Aires, Grupo Editor Latinoamericano.
Grugel, J. (1995) *Politics and Development in the Caribbean Basin*, London, Macmillan.
Guerra-Borges, A. (1991) *La integración de América Latina y el Caribe, México*, Instituto de Investigaciones Económicas, Universidad Autónoma de México.
Haas, E. (1964) *Beyond the Nation State*, Stanford, Stanford University Press.
Halliday, F. (1994) *Rethinking International Relations*, London, Macmillan.
Held, D. (ed.), (1991) *Political Theory Today*, Stanford, Stanford University Press.
Hennessy, A. (ed.), (1992) 'Intellectuals in the Twentieth-Century Caribbean' Vol. 1: *Spectre of the New Class – The Commonwealth Caribbean*, London, Macmillan.

Hennessy, A. (ed.), (1992) 'Intellectuals in the Twentieth-Century Caribbean' Vol 2: *Unity in Variety – the Hispanic and Francophone Caribbean*, London, Macmillan.
Hennessy, A. and Lambie, G. (eds), (1993) *The Fractured Blockade – West European-Cuban Relations During the Revolution*, London, Macmillan.
Hill, C. and Beshoff, P. (eds), (1994a) *Two Worlds of International Relations*, London, Routledge.
Hoffman, S. (1988) *Orden mundial o primacía. La política exterior nortemaricana desde la Guerra Fría*, Buenos Aires; Grupo Editor Latinoamericano.
Horsman, R. (1985) *La raza y el destino manifiesto. Orígenes del anglosajonismo racial norteamericano*, México, Fondo de Cultura Económica.
Hufbauer, G. C. and Schott, J. (1994) *Western Hemispheric Economic Integration*, Washington, Institute for International Economics.
Instituto Latinoamericano de Servicios Legales Alternativos (ILSA) (comp.), (1995) *Globalización, integración y derechos humanos en el Caribe*, Bogotá, ILSA.
Jackson, R. (1993) *Quasi-States: Sovereignty, International Relations and the Third World*, Cambridge, Cambridge University Press.
Jelin, E. and Hershberg, E. (eds), (1996) *Construir la democracia: derechos humanos, ciudadanía y sociedad en América Latina*, Caracas, Nueva Sociedad.
Juneje, R. (1996) *Caribbean Transactions – West Indian Culture in Literature*, London, Macmillan.
Keohane, R. (1988) *Después de la hegemonía. Cooperación y discordia en la política económica mundial*, Buenos Aires, Grupo Editor Latinoamericano.
Keohane, R. (ed.), (1986) *Neorealism and its Critics*, New York, Columbia University Press.
Keohane, R. and Nye, J. (1988) *Poder e interdependencia. La política mundial en transición*, Buenos Aires, Grupo Editor Latinoamericano.
Knight, F. and Palmer, C. (eds), (1989) *The Modern Caribbean*, Chapel Hill, The University of North Carolina Press.
Koningsbruggen, P. van (1996) *Trinidad Carnival: A Quest for National Identity*, London, Macmillan.
Krasner, S. (ed), (1983) *International Regimes*, Ithaca, Cornell University Press.
Krasner, S. (1989) *Conflicto estructural. El Tercer Mundo contra el liberalismo global*, Buenos Aires, Grupo Editor Latinoamericano.
Lalta, S. and Freckleton, M. (eds), (1993) *Caribbean Economic Development. The First Generation*, Kingston, Ian Randle Publishers.
Levine, B. (ed.), (1983) *The New Cuban Presence in the Caribbean*, Boulder, Westview.
Lipietz, A. (1989) *Towards a New Economic Order. Postfordism, Ecology and Democracy*, Cambridge, Polity Press.
Maingot, A. (1994a) *The United States and the Caribbean*. Boulder, Westview.
Mato, D. (ed.), (1994) *Teoría y política de la construcción de identidades y diferencias en América Latina y el Caribe*, Caracas, UNESCO/Nueva Sociedad.
McAfee, K. (1991) *Storm Signals. Structural Adjustment and Development Alternatives in the Caribbean*, Boston, South End Press/OXFAM America.
McGrew, A. G. and Lewis, P. G. et al., (1992) *Global Politics*, London, Polity Press.
Mitranyi, D. (1943) *A Working Peace System*, London, Royal Institute of International Affairs.
Moneta, C. and Quenan, C. (1994) *Las reglas de juego. América, globalización y regionalismo*, Buenos Aires, Corregidor.
Morgenthau, H. (1986) *Política entre las naciones. La lucha por el poder y la paz*, Buenos Aires, Grupo Editor Latinoamericano.

Muñoz, H. and Tulchin, J. (eds), (1984) *Entre la autonomía ya la subordinación. Política exterior de los países latinoamericanos*, Buenos Aires, Grupo Editor Latinoamericano.
Nicholls, D. (1996) *From Dessalines to Duvalier – Race, Colour and National Independence in Haiti 3rd Edition*, London, Macmillan.
ODCA/Fundación Konrad Adenauer (1994) *El Caribe frente al siglo XXI. Elementos de análisis*, Caracas.
Olson, W. and Groom, A. J. R. (1991) *International Relations Then and Now. Origins and Trends in Interpretation*, London, Harper Collins Academic.
Oostindie, G. (ed.), (1996) *Ethnicity in the Caribbean – Essays in Honor of Harry Hoetink*, London, Macmillan.
Palan, R. and Gills, B. (1994) *Transcending the State-Global Divide. A Neostructuralist Agenda in International Relations*, Boulder, Lynne Rienner.
Parker, R. (1988) *El sindicalismo cristiano latinoamericano*, Caracas, Consejo de Desarrollo Científico y Humanístico/Universidad Central de Venezuela.
Parry, G. (ed.), (1994) *Politics in an Interdependent World*, Cambridge, Edward Elgar.
Pastor, R. (1992) *Whirlpool – US Foreign Policy Toward Latin America and the Caribbean*, Princeton, Princeton University Press.
Payne, A. and Sutton, P. (eds), (1993) *Caribbean Modern Politics*, London, Macmillan.
Preeg, E. H. and Levine, J. D. (1994) *Cuba and the New Caribbean Economic Order*, Washington DC, The Center for Strategic and International Studies.
Ramsaran, R. (ed.), (1993) *Caribbean Economic Policy and South-South Co-operation: arising from the South Commission Report, The Challenge South*, London, Macmillan.
Rosenau, J. (1990) *Turbulence in World Politics*, Princeton, Princeton University Press.
Rosenau, J. and Czempiel, E. (eds) (1992) *Governance Without Government: Order and Change in World Politics*, Cambridge, Cambridge University Press.
Rosenau, P. M. (1992) *Post-Modernism and the Social Sciences, Insights, Inroads, and Intrusions*, Princeton, Princeton University Press.
Russell, R. (ed.), (1992) *Enfoques teóricos y metodológicos para el estudio de la política exterior*, Buenos Aires, RIAL/Grupo Editor Latinoamericano.
Sametband, M. J. (1994) *Entre el orden y el caos: la complejidad*, Buenos Aires, Fondo de Cultura Económica.
Sankatsing, G. (1994) *Las ciencias sociales en el Caribe*. Caracas, UNESCO/Nueva Sociedad.
Serbin, A. (1987) *Etnia, clase y nación en la cultura política del Caribe de habla inglesa*, Caracas, Ediciones de la Academia Nacional de la Historia.
Serbin, A. (1989a) *El Caribe: zona de paz?*, Caracas, Nueva Sociedad/Comisión Sudamericana de Paz.
Serbin, A. (1990) *Caribbean Geopolitics: Toward Security Through Peace?*, Boulder, Lynne Rienner.
Serbin, A. (ed.), (1993) 'La nueva agenda de seguridad en el Caribe', *Cuadernos del INVESP*, Caracas, No. 2, July-December.
Serbin, A. and Bryan, A. (eds), (1991) *¿Vecinos indiferentes? Las relaciones entre el Caribe de habla inglesa y América Latina*, Caracas, Nueva Sociedad/INVESP.
Serbin, A. and Bryan, A. (eds), (1991) *El Caribe hacia el año 2000*, Caracas, Nueva Sociedad.
Serbin, A. and Romero, C. (eds), (1993) *El Grupo de los Tres: asimetrías y convergencias*, Caracas, Nueva Sociedad/INVESP.
Serbin, A. and Tulchin, J. (eds), (1994) *El Caribe y Cuba en la Postguerra Fría*, Caracas, Nueva Sociedad/INVESP.

Sklair, L. (1991) *Sociology of the Global System*, Baltimore, The Johns Hopkins University Press.
Smith, A. (1991) *National Identity*, Reno, University of Nevada Press.
Smith, P. (ed.), (1993) *The Challenge of Integration. Europe and the Americas*, North-South Center, University of Miami/New Brunswick, Transaction Publishers.
Sojo, C. (1995) *El arbitrio del mercado*, San José de Costa Rica, Facultad Latinoamericana de Ciencias Sociales (FLACSO).
Stallings, B. (ed.), (1995) *Global Change, Regional Response. The New International Context of Development*, New York, Cambridge University Press.
Strange, S. (1988) *States and Markets*, London, Pinter Publishers.
Stubbs, R. and Underhill, G. R. D. (eds), (1994a) *Political Economy and the Changing Global Order*, London, Macmillan.
Tomassini, L. (1991) *La política internacional en un mundo postmoderno*, Buenos Aires, Grupo Editor Latinoamericano.
UNRISD (1995) *Estados de desorden. Los efectos sociales de la globalización*, Londres, Instituto de Investigaciones de las Naciones Unidas para el Desarrollo Social (UNRISD).
Walker, R. B. J. (1988) *One World, Many Worlds: Struggles for a Just World Peace*, Boulder, Lynne Rienner.
Wallerstein, I. (1988) *El capitalismo histórico*, México, Siglo XXI.
Wallerstein, I. (1995) *After Liberalism*, New York, The New Press.
Waltz, K. (1979) *Theory of International Relations*, New York, Random House.
Watson, H. (ed.), (1994) *The Caribbean in the Global Political Economy*, Boulder, Lynne Rienner.
Wedderburn, J. (ed.), (1990) *Integration and Participatory Development*, Bridgetown, FES/ACE.
Wight, M. (1977a) *Systems of States*, Leicester, Leicester University Press.
Wight, M. (1977b) *International Theory: The Three Traditions*, Leicester, Leicester University Press.
Williams, F. (1984) *La Internacional Socialista y América Latina. Una visión crítica*, Azcapotzalco, Universidad Autónoma Metropolitana.
Worrell, de L. and Bourne, C. (1989) *Economic Adjustment Policies for Small Nations. Theory and Experience in the English-Speaking Caribbean*, New York, Praeger.

Articles and papers

Aglietta, M. and Brender, A. (1994) 'La globalización financiera: fundamentos y consecuencias', Moneta and Quenan, op. cit., pp. 49–77.
Amin, S. (1994) 'El futuro de la polarización global', *Nueva Sociedad*, Caracas, No. 132, pp. 118–27.
Arriola, S. (1995) 'Las megatendencias de la economía internacional', *Capítulos del SELA*, Caracas, No. 43, April-June, pp. 89–95.
Bernard, M. (1994) 'Post-Fordism, Transnational Production, and the Changing Global Political Economy', Stubbs and Underhill, op. cit., pp. 216–29.
Biersteker, T. (1992) 'The "Triumph" of Neoclassical Economics in the Developing World: Policy Convergence and Bases of Governance in the International Economic Order', Rosenau and Czempiel, op. cit., pp. 102–31.
Bradford, C. (1994) 'Multeralismo, regionalismo y nuevo orden internacional: tendencias e implicaciones para América Latina y el Caribe', Moneta and Quenan, op. cit., pp. 127–46.

Braveboy-Wagner, J. (1995) 'The State and Status of Research on Caribbean International Relations', paper presented to the *XIX International Congress of the Latin American Studies Association*, Washington, September 28–30, 1995.

Broadbent, E. (1993) 'Democracy, Capitalism and Foreign Policy: Ten Propositions About the New World Order', *Canadian Foreign Policy*, Ottawa, Vol. 1, No. 2, Spring, pp. 1–12.

Brown, A. (1995) 'Caribbean Cultures and Mass Communication Technology Use: Challenges and Options', Dunn, H. (ed.) *Globalization, Communications and Caribbean Identity*, Kingston, Ian Randle Publishers, pp. 40–53.

Busch, M. and Milner, H. (1994) 'The Future of the International Trading System: International Firms, Regionalism and Domestic Politics', Stubbs and Underhill, op. cit., pp. 259–75.

Buttedabl, P. (1983) 'Evaluación a plazo medio del proyecto UNICA', *Caribbean Educational Bulletin*, San Juan, Vol. X, No. 3, September, pp. 5–68.

Buzan, B. (1991) 'New Patterns of Global Security in the Twenty First Century', *International Affairs*, Cambridge, Vol. 67, No. 3, July, pp. 431–51.

Buzan, B. (1993) 'From International System to International Society: Structural Realism and Regime Theory meet the English School', *International Organization*, Cambridge, 47, 3, Summer, pp. 327–52.

Caribbean Development Bank (1993) 'Adjustment Problems of CARICOM States' Lalta and Freckleton, op. cit., pp. 35–46.

Carrington, E. (1994) 'CARICOM y la Asociación de Estados del Caribe', *Política Internacional*, Caracas, No. 34, April-June, pp. 1–14.

Child, J. (1985) 'Variables para la política de Estados Unidos en la Cuenca del Caribe en la decada de 1980: seguridad', Greene and Scowcroft, op. cit., pp. 145–90.

Clarke, C. (1985) 'Caribbean Consciousness', Thomas-Hope, E. (ed.), *Perspectives on Caribbean Regional Identity*, Liverpool: Centre for Latin American Studies, University of Liverpool, Monograph Series No. 11.

CONAC (1991) 'Encuentro Nacional del Mundo Caribe', *Informe Final*, Caracas, Consejo Nacional de la Cultura (CONAC).

Cox, R. (1992) 'Towards a Post-Hegemonic Conceptualization of World Order: Reflections on the Relevancy of Ibn Khaldun', Rosenau and Czempiel, op. cit., pp. 132–59.

Cox, R. (1994) 'Global Restructuring: Making Sense of the Changing International Political Economy', Stubbs and Underhill, op. cit., pp. 45–59.

De la Ossa, A. (1996) 'Cuenca del Caribe: mecanismos para profundizar la participación de los actores sociales en el proceso de regionalización', paper presented to the Conference *La nueva agenda sociopolítica de la integración en el Gran Caribe*, INVESP/SELA, Caracas, 12–3 February 1996.

Del Arenal, C. (1990) 'La teoría de las relaciones internacionales hoy: debates y paradigmas', *Relaciones Internacionales*, San José de Costa Rica, 32–3, Third and Fourth Trimesters, pp. 9–20.

Diamond L. (1994) 'Toward Democratic Consolidation. Rethinking Civil Society', *Journal of Democracy*, pp. 4–17.

Dominguez, J. (1993) 'The Caribbean Question: Why Has Liberal Democracy (Surprisingly) Flourished?', Dominguez et al., op. cit., pp. 1–27.

Doñé Molina, E. (1991) 'Conciencia de género e identidad racial y caribeña en el Movimiento de Mujeres Dominicanas', paper presented to the *XVI Annual Conference of the Caribbean Studies Association*, La Habana, 21–4 May.

Drainville, André (1995) 'Of Social Spaces, Citizenship, and the Nature of Power in the World Economy', *Alternatives* (Victoria), No. 20, pp. 51–79.

Erisman, M. (1984) Preface to Erisman, M. (ed.), *The Caribbean Challenge. US Policy in a Volatile Region*, Boulder, Westview.
Erisman, M. (1995) 'Evolving Cuban-CARICOM Relations: A Comparative Cost/Benefit Analysis', *New West Indian Guide*, Leiden, Vol. 69 (1–2), pp. 45–65.
Erisman, M. and Martz, J. (eds), (1982) Preface to Erisman and Martz, *Colossus Challenged. The Struggle for Caribbean Influence*, Boulder, Lynne Rienner.
Falk, R. (1993) 'The Making of Global Citizenship', Brecher et al., op. cit., pp. 39–51.
Festival del Caribe (1993) 'World Congress on Death. Second Announcement', Santiago de Cuba, Casa del Caribe.
Gaztambide-Géigel, A. (1995) 'La invención del Caribe en el siglo XX. Las definiciones del Caribe como problema histórico y metodológico', paper presented to the *XX Annual Conference of the Caribbean Studies Association*, Curazao, 22–7 May.
Giacalone, R. (1995) 'El desarrollo institucional en el Caribe: desafío para la communidad académica y la Asociación de Estados del Caribe', presidential address to the *XX Annual Conference of the Caribbean Studies Association*, Curazao, 22–7 May.
Gill, H. (1993) 'The NAFTA Problematique and the Challenges for the Caribbean Community', paper presented to the Conference on *The Caribbean: Range of Choice for the 90s*, North-South Center, University of Miami, 10–1 September.
Gill, H. (1995) 'The Association of Caribbean States: Prospects for a "Quantum Leap"', *The North-South Agenda Papers*, No. 11, January, Miami, North-South Center.
Gill, H., Pellerano, F., Hess, R. (1995) 'A New Strategy to Promote Regional Integration in the Caribbean Region', draft report prepared on behalf of the European Commission, October.
Gill, S. (1994) 'Knowledge, Politics, and Neo-Liberal political Economy', Stubbs and Underhill, op. cit., pp. 75–86.
Girvan, N. (1990) 'Reflections on Regional Integration and Disintegration', Wedderburn, op. cit., pp. 1–6.
Goldstein, J. and Keohane, R. O. (1993) 'Ideas and Foreign Policy: An Analytical Framework', Goldstein and Keohane, op. cit., pp. 3–29.
Grabendorff, W. (1993) 'The Price of Integration: Reducing or Redefining State Sovereignty', Smith, P., op. cit., pp. 339–60.
Griffith, I. (1995) 'The Money Laundering Dilemma in the Caribbean', *Cuadernos de Trabajo Río Piedras*, No. 4, September, Instituto de Estudios del Caribe, Universidad de Puerto Rico.
Griffith, I. and Munroe, T. (1995) 'Drugs and Democracy in the Caribbean', *The Journal of Commonwealth and Comparative Politics*, London, Vol. XXXIII, No. 3, November, pp. 357–76.
Groom, A. J. R. (1988) 'Practitioners and Academics: Towards a Happier Relationship?', Banks, M. (ed.), *Conflict in World Society. A New Perspective on International Relations*, Brighton, Wheatsheaf Books Ltd, pp. 192–207.
Grupo de Trabajo del Consejo Atlántico sobre la Cuenca del Caribe (1985) 'Intereses Occidentales y opciones políticas de los EEUU en la Cuenca del Caribe: documentos sobre política', Greene and Scowcroft, op. cit., pp. 13–65.
Haas, P. M. (1992) 'Introduction: epistemic communities and international policy coordination', *International Organization*, Cambridge, Vol. 46, No. 1, Winter, pp. 1–35.
Hall, J. A. (1993) 'Ideas and the Social Sciences', Goldstein and Keohane, op. cit., pp. 31–53.
Harker, T. (1990) 'Un desarrollo sostenido para el Caribe', *Revista de la CEPAL*, Santiago de Chile, No. 41, August. Reproduced in *Síntesis*, Madrid, No. 17, May–August 1992, pp. 171–94.

Harker, T. (1994) 'Caribbean Economic Performance in the 1990s: Implications for Future Policy', Watson, op. cit., pp. 9–27.
Hein, W. (1994) 'El fin del Estado-nación y el nuevo orden mundial', *Nueva Sociedad*, Caracas, No. 132, July-August, pp. 82–99.
Held, D. (1991) 'Democracy, the Nation-State and the Global System', Held, op. cit., pp. 197–235.
Helleiner, E. (1994) 'From Bretton Woods to Global Finance: A World Turned Upside down', Stubbs and Underhill, op. cit., pp. 163–75.
Hill, C. and Beshoff, P. (1994b) 'The two worlds: natural partnership or necessary distance?' Hill and Beshoff, op. cit., pp. 211–25.
Hillcoat, G. and Quenan, C. (1991) 'Restructuración internacional y respecialización productiva en el Caribe', Serbin and Bryan op. cit., pp. 103–37.
Huber, E. (1993) 'The Future of Democracy in the Caribbean', Dominguez et al., op. cit., pp. 74–96.
Huntington, S. (1993) 'The Clash of Civilizations?', *Foreign Affairs*, Vol. 72, No. 3, Summer, pp. 24–48.
Hurrell, A. (1992) 'Latin America in the New World Order: A Regional Bloc for Latin America?', *International Affairs*, London, Vol. 68, No. 1, January, pp. 121–39.
Hurrell, A. and Woods, N. (1995) 'Globalisation and Inequality', *Millenium*, London, Winter, Vol. 24, No. 3, pp. 447–70.
Hutchinson, G. and Schumacher, U. (1994) 'NAFTA's Threat to Central American and Caribbean Basin Exports: A Revealed Comparative Advantage Approach', *Journal of Interamerican Studies and World Affairs*, Miami, Vol. 36, No. 1, Spring, pp. 127–49.
Jácome, F. (1992) 'Las relaciones entre América Latina, el Caribe y Europa: la influencia de los factores etnorraciales', *Síntesis*, Madrid, No. 17, May-August, pp. 35–46.
Jácome, F. (1993) 'Identidad étnica y proyectos políticos: influencia de los factores etnorraciales', Jácome, F. (ed), *Diversidad cultural y tensión regional: América Latina y el Caribe*, Caracas, INVESP/Nueva Sociedad, pp. 11–20.
Jácome, F. (1994) 'Identidades nacionales y cooperación en la región del Caribe', Mato, op. cit., pp. 243–50.
Jácome, F. and Sankatsing, G. (1992) 'La cooperación ambiental en el Caribe: actores principales', Serbin, A. (ed.), *Medio ambiente, seguridad y cooperación regional en el Caribe*, Caracas, CIQRO/INVESP/Nueva Sociedad.
Kaiser, K. (1994) 'North America and the Caribbean Basin: Viable Paths to a Greater North American Market', *North American Forum*, Working Paper No. 94/1, Conference Report, January 14–16, Littlefield Center, Stanford University.
Keck, M. and Sikkink, K. (1994) 'Transnational Issue Networks in International Politics', ms.
King, C. (1994) 'Post-Sovietology: area studies or social science?', *International Affairs*, London, Vol. 70, No. 2, April, pp. 291–7.
Latorre, E. (1982) 'Strengthening UNICA', *Caribbean Educational Bulletin*, San Juan, Vol. IX, No. 3, pp. 2–15.
Lewis, D. (1990) 'Non-Governmental Organizations and Alternative Strategies: Bridging the Development Gap between Central America and the Caribbean', Wedderburn, op. cit.
Lewis, D. (1991) 'El sector informal y los nuevos actores sociales en el desarrollo del Caribe', Serbin and Bryan, op. cit.
Lewis, D. (1994) 'Non-governmental Organizations and Caribbean Development', *Annals*, Washington, 533, May, pp. 128–38.

Lewis, D. (1995) 'La experiencia de la integración regional en el Caribe: un análisis prospectivo', paper presented to the conference *Hacia una agenda sociopolítica de la integración en el Caribe*, Santo Domingo, March 1–3.
Lewis, L. (1994) 'Restructuring and Privatization in the Caribbean', Watson, op. cit., pp. 173–90.
Lewis, L. and Nurse, L. (1994) 'Caribbean Trade Unionism and Global Restructuring', Watson, op. cit., pp. 191–206.
Linklater, A. (1992) 'The Question of the Next Stage in International Relations Theory: A Critical-Theoretical Point of View', *Millenium*, London, Vol. 21, No. 1, Spring, pp. 77–100.
Lipietz, A. (1994) 'The National and the Regional: Their Autonomy vis-a-vis the Capitalist World Crisis', Palan and Gills, op. cit., pp. 23–44.
Macdonald, L. (1994) 'Globalizing Civil Society: Interpreting International NGOs in Central America', *Millenium*, London, Summer, Vol. 23, No. 2, pp. 267–85.
Mace, G., Bélanger, L. and Thérien, J. P. (1993) 'Regionalism in the Americas and the Hierarchy of Power', *Journal of Interamerican Studies and World Affairs*, Miami, Summer, Vol. 35, No. 2, pp. 115–57.
Maingot, A. (1983a) 'Caribbean Studies as Area Studies: Past Performances and Recent Stirrings', *Caribbean Educational Bulletin*, San Juan, Vol. x, No. 1, January, pp. 1–14.
Maingot, A. (1983b) 'Cuba and the Commonwealth Caribbean: Playing the Cuban card', Levine, op. cit., pp. 19–42.
Maingot, A. (1994b) 'A Region Becoming: Historical Conjuncture and Ideology in the Shaping of Caribbean politics', paper presented to the ODCA Conference *El Caribe frnet al Siglo XXI*, Aruba, 9–10 September.
Martin, A. (1994) 'Labour, the Keynesian Welfare and the Changing International Political Economy', Stubbs and Underhill, op. cit., pp. 60–74.
Mato, D. (1994) 'Teoria y política de la construcción de identidades y diferencias en América Latina y el Caribe', Mato, op. cit., pp. 13–29.
McGrew, A. G. (1992a) 'Conceptualizing Global Politics', McGrew et al., op. cit., pp. 1–28.
McGrew, A. G. (1992b) 'Global Politics in a Transnational Era', McGrew et al., op. cit., pp. 313–30.
Menzel, U. (1994) 'Tras el fracaso de la grandes teorías, que será del Tercer Mundo?', *Nueva Sociedad*, Caracas, No. 132, July-August, pp. 66–79.
Mitranyi, D. (1965) 'The Prospect for Integration: Federal or Functional?', *Journal of Common Market Studies*, 4 (2).
Mols, M. (1993) 'The Integration Agenda: A Framework for Comparison', Smith, P., op. cit., pp. 51–7.
Moller Okin, S. (1991) 'Gender, the Public and the Private', Held, op. cit., pp. 67–90.
Moneta, C. (1994) 'El proceso de globalización: percepciones y desarrollos', Moneta and Quenan, op. cit., pp. 147–65.
Neufeld, M. (1993) 'Reflexivity and International Relations Theory', *Millenium*, London, Vol. 22, No. 1, Spring, pp. 53–75.
Neureither, K. (1994) 'The syndrome of democratic deficit in the European Community', Parry, op. cit., pp. 94–110.
Palan, R. (1994) 'State and Society in International Relations', Palan and Gills, op. cit., pp. 45–61.
Parry, G. (1994b) 'Political life in an interdependent world', Parry, op. cit., pp. 1–19.
Payne, A. (1993) 'Westminster Adapted: The Political Order of the Commonwealth Caribbean', Dominguez et al., op. cit., pp. 57–73.

Pinder, J. (1994) 'Interdependence, democracy and federalism', Parry, op. cit., pp. 111–25.
Powell, R. (1994) 'Anarchy in international relations debate: the neorealist-neoliberal debate', *International Organization*, Cambridge, 48, 3, Spring, pp. 313–44.
Putnam, R. D. (1988) 'Diplomacy and domestic politics: the logic of two-level games', *International Organization*, Cambridge, 42, 3, Summer, pp. 427–60.
Quick, S. (1993) 'The International Economy and the Caribbean: The 1990s and Beyond', Dominguez et al., op. cit., pp. 212–28.
Risse-Kappen, T. (1994) 'Ideas do not float freely: transnational coalitions, domestic structures, and the end of the Cold War', *International Organization*, Cambridge, 48, 2, Spring, pp. 185–214.
Rogalski, M. (1994) 'El auge de la fractura Norte-Sur. ¿es posible un gobierno global?', *Nueva Sociedad*, Caracas, No. 132, July-August, pp. 100–17.
Rosati, J. A., Carroll, D. J. and Crate, R. A. (1990) 'A Critical Assessment of the Power of Human Needs in World Society', Burton and Dukes, op. cit.
Rosenau, J. (1992a) 'Governance, order and change in world politics', Rosenau and Czempiel, op. cit., pp. 1-29.
Rosenau, J. (1992b) 'Citizenship in a Changing Global Order', Rosenau and Czempiel, op. cit., pp. 272–94.
Rosenau, J. (1992c) 'The United Nations in a Turbulent World', *International Peace Academy/Occasional Paper Series*, Boulder, Lynne Rienner.
Rosenthal, G. (1993) 'Treinta años de integración en América Latina: un análisis crítico', *Estudios Internacionales*, Santiago de Chile, año XXVI, January-March, No. 101, pp. 74–88.
Russell, R. (1992) 'Introduccion', Russell, op. cit., pp. 7–18.
Serbin, A. (1989b) 'Identidad cultural y desarrollo en el Caribe angófono: algunas reflexiones desde una visión antropológica', Bansart, op. cit., pp. 43–60.
Serbin, A. (1994a) 'Transnational Relations and Regionalism in the Caribbean', *Annals*, Washington, 533, May, pp. 139–50.
Serbin, A. (1994b) 'Integración y relaciones transnacionales: el entramado social del proceso de regionalización en la Cuenca del Caribe', *Perfiles Latinoamericanos*, México, 3, No. 4, pp. 7–36.
Serbin, A. (1994c) 'Reconfiguraciones geoeconómicas y transiciones políticas en el Caribe de los noventa', Serbin and Tulchin, op. cit., pp. 11–25.
Serbin, A. (1994d) '¿Una reconfiguración de la Cuenca del Caribe?', *Nueva Sociedad*, Caracas, No. 133, September-October, pp. 20–6.
Shaw, M. (1994) 'Civil Society and Global Politics: Beyond a Social Movements Approach', *Millenium*, London, Vol. 23, No. 3, pp. 647–67.
Sikkink, K. (1993) 'Human Rights, Principled Issue-Networks, and Sovereignty in Latin America', *International Organization*, Cambridge, 47, 3, Summer, pp. 411–41.
Smith, D. (1993) 'Central American and Caribbean People: Challenges and Needs During the 1990s', paper presented to the *IV Conference of the Association of the Caribbean Economists*, Curazao, 22–25 June.
Stallings, B. (1995) 'Introduction: global change, regional response', Stallings, op. cit., pp. 1–32.
Strange, S. (1994a) 'Global government and global opposition', Parry, op. cit., pp. 20–33.
Strange, S. (1994b) 'Rethinking Structural Change in the International Political Economy: States, Firms and Diplomacy', Stubbs and Underhill, op. cit., pp. 103–15.
Stubbs, R. and Underhill, G. R. D. (1994b) 'Global Issues in Historical Perspective', Stubbs and Underhill, op. cit., pp. 145–62.

Stubbs, R. and Underhill, G. R. D. (1994c) 'Global Trends, Regional Patterns', Stubbs and Underhill, op. cit., pp. 331–5.
Stubbs, R. and Underhill, G. R. D. (1994d) 'State Policies and Global Changes', Stubbs and Underhill, op. cit., pp. 421–3.
Suarez, L. (1995) 'Nuevo "orden" mundial, integración y derechos humanos en el Caribe: apuntes para una reconceptualización', *Globalización integración y derechos humanos en el Caribe*, Bogotá, Instituto Latinoamericano de Servicios Legales Alternativos, (ILSA).
Thomas, C. (1979) 'Neocolonialism and Caribbean Integration', Ince, B. (ed.), *Contemporary International Relations in the Caribbean*, St. Augustine, Institute of International Relations, UWI.
Tomassini, L. (1989) 'Estructura y funcionamiento del sistema internacional y sus repercusiones sobre la solución de conflictos, especialmente en países pequeños y medianos', *Integración solidaria para el mantenimiento de la paz en América Latina*, Caracas, Universidad Simón Bolivar/Organización de Estados Americanos, (USB).
Tooze, R. (1992) 'Conceptualizing the Global Economy', McGrew et al., op. cit., pp. 233–49.
Tooze, R. (1994) 'International political economy and the national policy-maker', Hill and Beshoff, op. cit., pp. 54–76.
Underhill, G. (1994) 'Conceptualizing the changing global order', Stubbs and Underhill, op. cit., pp. 17–44.
UNICA (1983) 'Informe de la reunión de UNICA celebrada en Barbados', *Caribbean Educational Bulletin*, San Juan, Vol. X, No. 1, pp. 29–38.
Van Klaveren, A. (1984) 'El análisis de la política exterior latinoamericana. Perspectivas teóricas', Muñoz and Tulchin, op. cit., pp. 14–50.
Van Klaveren, A. (1992) 'Entendiendo las políticas exteriores latinoamericanas: modelo para armar', *Estudios Internacionales*, Santiago de Chile, año XXV, No. 98, April-June, pp. 169–215.
Vilas, C. (1994) 'La hora de la sociedad civil', *Análisis Politico*, Bogotá, No. 21, January-April, pp. 5–13.
Von Beyme, K. (1994) 'Approaches to a theory of the transformation to democracy and market society', Parry, op. cit., pp. 126–45.
Wallace, W. (1994) 'Between two worlds: think-tanks and foreign policy', Hill and Beshoff, op. cit., pp. 139–62.
Wàterman, P. (1994) 'Global, civil, solidario. La complejización del nuevo mundo', *Nueva Sociedad*, Caracas, No. 132, pp. 128–45.
Watson, H. (1994a) 'Introduction: The Caribbean and the Techno-Paradigm Shift in Global Capitalism', Watson, op. cit., pp. 1–8.
Watson, H. (1994b) 'Beyond Nationalism: Caribbean Options under Global Capitalism', Watson, op. cit., pp. 225–31.
Watson, H. (1994c) 'State/Nation-State, Neoliberalism and Restructuring: Global Issues in Caribbean Reality', paper presented to the *International Studies Association* Conference, Washington DC, March 28–April 1.
Weber, C. (1994) 'Good Girls, Little Girls and Bad Girls: Male Paranoia in Robert Keohane's Critique on Feminist International Relations', *Millenium*, London, Vol. 23, No. 2, Summer, pp. 337–49.
Weelhausen, E. J. (1984) 'A Report of his Mission to the Caribbean', *Caribbean Educational Bulletin*, San Juan, Vol. XI, No. 2, pp. 3–56.
Wendt, A. E. (1987) 'The Agent-Structure Problem in International Relations Theory', *International Organization*, Cambridge, 41, 3, Summer, pp. 339–70.

Whiting, Van R. (1993) 'The Dynamics of Regionalization: Road Map to the Open Future?', Smith, P., op. cit., pp. 17–50.
Wood, B. (1974) 'Areas, estudio', *Enciclopedia Internacional de las Ciencias Sociales*, Vol. 1, Madrid, Aguilar, pp. 524–30.
Worrell, D. (1993) 'The Economies of the English-speaking Caribbean since 1960', Dominguez et al., op. cit., pp. 189–221.

Documents

Assembly of Caribbean People (1994) *Hacia una agenda popular para la soberanía del Caribe y el bienestar del pueblo caribeño*, Mimeo, August.
Association of Caribbean States (1994a) *Documentos preparatorios de la reunión de Caracas*, June 29.
Association of Caribbean States (1994b) *Constitutive Agreement of the Association of Caribbean States*, Cartagena de Indias, July 24.
Association of Caribbean Economists (1988) *Constitution of the Association of Caribbean Economists*, Mimeo, March.
Caribbean Basin Technical Advisory Group (1991) *Memorandum on Central American/Caribbean Cooperation*, Mimeo, September.
Caribbean Council for Europe (1993) *Communiqué of the Sixth Europe/Caribbean Conference*, Santo Domingo, November 10–12.
CARICOM (1993) *Proposed Plan of Action for the Establishment of an Association of Caribbean States*, Barbados, December.
CEPAL (1994a) *El regionalismo abierto en América Latina y el Caribe*, LC/L.808 (CEG.19/3), January 13.
CEPAL (1994b) *Desarrollo reciente de los procesos de integración en América Latina y el Caribe*, LC/R.1381, May 5.
CEPAL (1994c) *La nueva integración regional en el marco de la ALADI*, LC/R.1403, June 30.
CEPAL (1994d) *El dinamismo reciente del comercio intrarregional de la Asociación Latinoamericana de Integración (ALADI)*, LC/R1436, August 23.
C/LAA (1991a) *Statement of the Subcommittee on Trade for the United States House of Representatives Ways and Means Committee*, February 28.
C/LAA (1991b) *A New Direction for the Nineties*, Mimeo, Washington.
Comisión Centroamericana de Ambiente y Desarrollo (1994) *Alianza centroamericana para el desarrollo sostenible*, Guácimo, Costa Rica.
COPPPAL (1991) *Reunión plenaria de la Comisión Permanente de Relaciones Económicas Internacionales*, Mimeo, Santiago de Chile.
COPPPAL (1992a) *Informe de actividades. Síntesis*, Mimeo, San Angel Inn, México.
COPPPAL (1992b) *Integración deuda externa y relaciones económicas internacionales*, Lima, Cambio y Desarrollo.
CRIES (1991) *Crisis, Challenges and Opportunities. The Caribbean in the 1990's*, Background Discussion Paper, Fourth CRIES General Assembly, La Habana, May 24.
CRIES (1992) *Propuesta de plan de trabajo para la subsede regional de CRIES en el Caribe*, Mimeo, December.
ECLAC/UN (1992) *Latin American and Caribbean Relations*, LC/G1725 (SES 24/17), April.
PARLATINO (1992) *Anuario del Parlamento Latinoamericano 1992*, Caracas, Sarbo.

SELA (1993) *Escenarios de cambio mundial*, XIX Reunión Ordinaria del Consejo Latinoamericano. Caracas, 25–9 October, SP/CL/XIX.O/DT No. 13.

SELA (1994a) *Informe de la reunión de expertos para el análisis de escenarios a largo plazo*, XX Reunión Ordinaria del Consejo Latinoamericano, México, DF, May 30–June 3, SP/CL/XX.O/Di No. 9.

SELA (1994b) *Perspectivas para la cooperación hemisférica entre América latina y el Caribe con Estados Unidos y Canadá*, Río de Janeiro, September 9–10, VIII Río Group Summit.

SELA (1994c) *El SELA ante los 'nuevos temas' del comercio internacional. Ideas para la acción*, Río de Janeiro, September 9–10, VIII Río Group Summit.

SELA (1994d) *América Latina y el Caribe: los compromisos de la Ronda Uruguay*, Río de Janeiro, September 9–10, VIII Río Group Summit, SP/CL/XX.O/Di No. 7.

SELA (1994e) *Evolución del proceso de integración regional (1993–4)*, XX Reunión Ordinaria del Consejo Latinoamericano, México, DF, May 30–June 3, SP/CL/XX.O/Di No. 7.

SELA (1995) *Relaciones comerciales en el siglo XXI: Los retos que enfrenta la ACS*, August.

SICA (1993a) *El sistema de integración centroamericana*, El Salvador, SG-SICA.

SICA (1993b) *La Centroamérica de Hoy*, El Salvador, SG-SICA.

UNDP (1994) 'Human Development Report', reproduced in SELA *Notas Estratégicas*, No. 5, June 1994.

UN ECLAC/CDCC (1994) *The World Summit for Social Development: A Caribbean Perspective*, LC/CAR/G.430, November 14.

West Indian Commission (WIC) (1992) *Time for Action*, Bridgeport, WIC.

World Bank (1994) *Caribbean region: Coping with Changes in the External Environment*, Report No. 12821 LAC, March 16.

Periodicals

Boletín de la Asociación de Economistas del Caribe (AEC) (1996), No. 3, January.
Caribbean Action (1991) Washington, Vol. VII, No. 1, October.
Caribbean Agenda (CA) (1991a) London, Vol. 1, No. 1, September.
Caribbean Agenda (CA) (1991b) London, Vol. 1, No. 2, December.
Caribbean Agenda (CA) (1992a) London, Vol. 1, No. 3, March.
Caribbean Agenda (CA) (1992b) London, Vol. 1, No. 4, June.
Caribbean Agenda (CA) (1992c) London, Vol. 1, No. 5, September.
Caribbean Agenda (CA) (1992d) London, Vol. 1, No. 6, December.
Caribbean Dialogue (CD) (1994), Vol. 1, No. 3, November-December.
Caribbean Dialogue (CD) (1995), Vol. 1, No. 4, January-February.
Caribbean Update (CU) (1991a), Vol. 7, No. 6, July.
Caribbean Update (CU) (1991b), Vol. 7, No. 10, November.
Caribbean Update (CU) (1992), Vol. 8, No. 2, March.
Caribbean Update (CU) (1995), Vol. 11, No. 10.
Hoja CEDEE (1991) año V, No. 10, September.
Panorama Centroamericano (PC) (1995a), No. 56, March-April.
Panorama Centroamericano (PC) (1995b), No. 57–8, May-June and July-August.
Revista Venezolano de Economía y Ciencias Sociales (1995), Caracas, UCV, No. 4, October-December.

Index

Figures in *italics* indicate tables.

Afro-Central America, 37
Andean Pact, 54, 80, 107
Anguilla, *60–2*, 72
Antigua and Barbuda, *60–2*, *84–5*
Arriola, Salvador, 28
Aruba, 27, 87, 95
Asia-Pacific rim/region, 8, 47
Asociación Latinoamericana de Integración (ALADI), 80, 107
Asociación Mexicana de Estudios Caribeños, 95
Asociación Venezolana de Estudios Caribeños (AVECA), 95
Assembly of Caribbean People, 91
Association of Caribbean Economists (ACE), 93, 94
Association of Caribbean States (ACS), 1, 36, 42, 43, 44, 54, 57, 59, *60–2*, 71–6, *72*, *75*, 78–82, *84–5*, 96, 97, 103–10, 112
Association of Research Institutes and Universities of the Caribbean (UNICA), 92, 93

Bahamas, *60–2*, *75*, *84–5*
Barbados, *60-2*, 74, *75*, *84–5*, 91, 92
Barbados Labour Party (BLP), 87
Belize, 34, 38, *60–2*, *75*, *84–5*
Benitez Rojo, Antonio, 33, 37
Black Muslims, 58–9
Black Power, 86
Bolivia, 107
Borges, Jorge Luis, 33
Brazil, 26, 79, 80, 107
Bretton Woods system, 48
British Empire, 15
Buenos Aires, 95
Bull, Hedley, 13
Bush, George, 73

Caldera, President, 79
Canada, 80, 89, 107
Canadian Cooperation Programme for the Caribbean (CARIBCAN), 56, 64, 105

Caracas, 95
Cardosa, President, 80
Caribbean Association for Feminist Research and Action (CAFRA), 91, 92
Caribbean Association of Industry and Commerce (CAIC), 88, 89
Caribbean Basin
 and the ACS, 71
 definitions, 36–40
 trade indicators, *84–5*
Caribbean Basin Initiative (CBI), 37–8, 41, 56, 64, 79
Caribbean Community (CARICOM), 11, 39, 43, 54, *60–2*, 71–9, *72*, 81, *84–5*, 91, 92, 105, 109
Caribbean Conservationist Association (CCA), 92
Caribbean Council of Churches (CCC), 90
Caribbean Council for Europe (CCE), 88
Caribbean Development Policy Center (CDPC), 83
Caribbean Environmental Health Institute (CEHI), 92
Caribbean Network for Integrated Rural Development (CNIRD), 91
Caribbean (NGO) Policy Development Center (CPDC), 91
Caribbean People's Development Agency (CARIPEDA), 90
Caribbean Studies, 94
Caribbean Studies Association (CSA), 93–4
Caribbean Studies Newsletter, 94
Caribbean Trade Advisory Group (CARIBTAG), 88
Caribbean/Central American Action Group (CCAA), 88–9
Caribbean/Latin American Action Group (C/LAA), 89
CARICOM *see* Caribbean Community
CARIFESTA, 43, 91
CARIFORUM, 44, 77
Cayman Islands, *60–2*, *72*
CBI, *see* Caribbean Basin Initiative

133

Index

Central America, 11, 34, 35, 37, 38, 39, 42, 56, *60–2*, 65, 71, *72*, 76, 77, 79, 86–7, 105, 109
Central American Common Market (CACM), 44, 71, 73, *84–5*
Central American Economic System (CAES), 44, 54
Central American Integration System (SICA), 73, 77
Central American Parliament, 11
Centre Nationale pour la Recherche Scientifique (CNRS), 25
Centres d'Etudes pour les Relations Internationales (CERI), 25
Centro de Estudios de América (CEA), 95
Chiapas rebellion, 67
Chile, 26, 107
Christian Democrat Organisation of Latin America (ODCA), 87
Clarke, Colin, 34
Clinton, President Bill, 80, 107
Colombia, 27, 38, 39, 59, *60–2*, 64, 65, 71, 73, 74, *75*, 76, 77, 79, *84–5*, 89, 94, 107
Colosío (Mexican presidential candidate), 67
Columbus, Christopher, 36
Commission for Development and Cooperation in the Caribbean (CDCC), 83
Consortium of Caribbean Universities for the Administration of Natural Resources, 92
Contadora Group, 72, 76
Coordinadora Regional de Institutos de Investigaciónes Económicas y Sociales (CRIES), 93, 94
Costa Rica, *60–2*, *75*, 77, *84–5*
Cuba, 27, 37–40, 56, 57, *60–2*, 65, 72, 73, 74, *75*, 77–80, *84–5*, 86, 87, 91, 92, 105, 106, 109, 110
'Cuban card', 56, 105
Curacao, 88, 92, 94

Decade of the Woman 1975–1985 (United Nations), 91
Development Alternatives with Women for a New Era (DAWN), 92
Dominica, *60–2*, *75*, *84–5*
Dominican Republic, 34, *60–2*, 63, 72, 73, 74, *75*, 77, 78, *84–5*, 86, 87, 88, 92, 94, 95, 105, 110
Dutch Guiana, 34, 38

Eastern Europe, 47
Economic Commission for Latin America and the Caribbean

(ECLAC) (CEPAL in Spanish), 10, 26, 27, 39, 40, 54, 83, 88
El Salvador, 38, *60–2*, *75*, *84–5*
Europe/Caribbean Conferences, 88
European Community/Union (EC/EU), 8, 47, 52–3, 56, 64, 73, 80, 88, 97, 108, 110, 112
European Parliament, 112

Facultad Latinoamericana de Ciencias Sociales (FLACSO), 95
Federación de Entidades Privadas de Centro America y Panamá (FEDEPRICAP), 89
Fordist Taylor model, 47
France, 25, 73, 109
francophonie, 25
Frankfurt school, 18
Free Trade Area of the Americas (FTAA), 79, 108
French Guiana, 27, 34, 38, *60–2*, *72*

General Agreement on Trade and Tariffs (GATT), 53
Germany, 24
Gill, Henry, 81
Goldstein, J., 21
Gramsci, Antonio, 17, 51
Great Britain, 24, 25, 27, 39, 73, 109
Grenada, 40, *60–2*, *75*, *84–5*, 86, 87
Group of Rio, 54, 80, 107
Group of Three (G-3), 44, 54, *60–2*, 64, 71–4, *72*, 76, 77, 78, *84–5*, 105, 109
Guadeloupe, 27, *60–2*, *72*, 91
Guianas, 34, 38
Guyana, 40, *60–2*, *75*, *84–5*, 86

Habermas, 18
Haiti, 34, 39, 57, *60–2*, 73, *75*, 77, *84–5*, 86, 87, 110
Havana, 95
Helms, Senator Jesse, 80
Helms-Burton Law, 56, 77, 80
Hispaniola, 34
Hobbes, Thomas, 13
Holland, 73, 109
Honduras, *60–2*, *75*, *84–5*

Initiative for the Americas (IFA), 72
Institut Français des Relations Internationales (IFRI), 25
Institute of Caribbean Studies (University of Puerto Rico), 94
Institute of International Relations, University of the West Indies, 26–7
Institute of Social and Economic Studies (University of the West Indies), 94

Institute of World Economy and
    International Relations, 26
Instituto Venezolano de Estudios
    Sociales y Politicos (INVESP), 92,
    95
International Socialist (IS), 86–7

Jamaica, 40, *60–2*, 63, *75*, *84–5*, 86, 90,
    94
Japan, 8, 47, 53, 105
Joint Economic Commission, 77

Keohane, R. O., 14, 21

Latin America, 8, 9–10, 17, 22, 26, 27,
    36, 37, 38, 40, 54, 55, 56, *60–2*,
    67–8, 72, 86, 87, 88, 94, 95, 113
Latin American Council of Social
    Sciences (CLACSO), 93, 95
Latin American Economic System
    (SELA), 39, 44, 52, *75*, *84–5*
Latin American Parliament, 87
League of Nations, 13
Levi-Strauss, Claude, 25
Lomé agreements, 56, 64, 77, 88, 105

Manley, Michael, 86
Martinique, 27, *60–2*, 72, 91
Marxism/neo-Marxism, 16, 17, 24, 25,
    26, 41, 86
Mercado Común Centroamericano
    (MERCOSUR), 54, 76, 79, 80,
    107
Mexico, 27, 38, 39, 54–5, 59, *60–2*, 64,
    65, 67, 71, 73, *75*, 76, 79–80, *84–5*,
    87, 89, 91, 94, 95, 107, 109
Miami Summit, 80, 107, 108
Montserrat, *60–2*, 72, *84–5*

National Businessmen's Council of
    the Dominican Republic (CNHE),
    88
National Trade Union Council of
    Trinidad and Tobago, 91
Netherlands Antilles, 27, *60–2*, 72, 87
New Jewel Movement, 86
New World Economic Order (NWEO),
    39
New World Group, 26
NGO Regional Forum on the GATT
    (1994), 91
Nicaragua, 40, *60–2*, *75*, *84–5*, 86, 94
North America, 8, 73, 105, 107
North American Free Trade Agreement
    (NAFTA), 45, 47, 53, 64, 72, 76, 77,
    79, 80, 81, 107, 109, 112
North–South, 16, 17

Organization of American States (OAS),
    44
OXFAM, 83

Panama, *60–2*, *75*, *84–5*
Partido Revolucionario Institucional
    (PRI), 65, 87
Pensamiento propio journal, 94
People's National Party (PNP), 86
Pérez, President Carlos Andrés, 79
Permanent Commission of Latin American
    Political Parties (COPPPAL), 87
Port-of-Spain summit meeting (ACS)
    (1995), 81, 107, 108
Post-Fordist model, 47, 48–9
Private Sector Organisation of Jamaica
    (PSOJ), 88
Puerto Rico, 27, 39, *60–2*, 63, *72*, 74, 81,
    90, 92, 93, 94, 95

Reagan, Ronald, 87
Rosenau, J., 5–7, 16, 52

St Martin, 34
St Kitts-Nevis, *60–2*, *75*, *84–5*
St Lucia, *60–2*, *75*, *84–5*
St Vincent and the Grenadines, *60–2*, *75*,
    84–5
San Jose dialogue, 105
San Juan, 95
Sandinistas, 56, 86
Santo Domingo, 77, 87, 88, 94
Second World War, 4, 37
Secretariat for Central American
    Economic Integration (SIECA),
    71–2, 77
SELA *see* Latin American Economic
    System
SICA *see* Central American Integration
    System
Simón Bolívar University of Venezuela,
    92
Social and Economic Studies, 94
South America, 38, 39, 107
South American Free Trade Area
    (SAFTA), 45, 80, 107
South–South cooperation, 39
Southeast Asia, 53, 73, 105
Southern Cone, 107
Soviet bloc, collapse of, 41, 86
Soviet Union, 25, 38, 40, 56, 57, 106
Stockholm Social Development
    Summit, 6
Suriname, 40, *60–2*, 73, *75*, *84–5*, 86

Third World, 6, 37, 39, 40, 42, 71, 87, 92,
    104

Torricelli amendment, 56
Trinidad and Tobago, 39, 59, *60–2*, 74, 75, *84–5*, 90
Turks and Caicos Islands, *60–2*, 72

UNESCO, 83
United Kingdom, *60–2, 72*
United Nations (UN), 91
United Nations Programme for the Environment (UNEP), 83
United States of America (US), 13, 15, 24, 25, 27, 37–41, 56, 57, *60–2*, 71, 72, 73, 77, 79, 80, 81, 87, 89, 93, 107, 108, 110
Universities of the West Indies, 27, 39, 92
University of Puerto Rico, 95

Venezuela, 27, 38, 39, 59, *60–2*, 64, 65, 67, 71, 73, 74, *75*, 76–7, 79, 80, *84–5*, 89, 91, 93, 94, 95, 107
Virgin Islands, *60–2, 72*, 81, 92, 95

Waltz, Kenneth, 13
Washington consensus, 54
West Indian Commission, 74, 75
West Indian Committee (WIC), 88, 97
Williams, Sir Eric, 39
Women and Development (WAND), 83, 91
Working Group on International Relations in the Caribbean Basin, 93, 94–5
World Trade Organisation (WTO), 53